W9-BMQ-325

Traffic Ticket Defense

Mark D. Sutherland, Esq.
Christopher J. Sutherland

Bonus Books, Inc., Chicago

©1993 by Bonus Books, Inc.
All Rights Reserved

Except for appropriate use in critical reviews or works of scholarship, the repro-
duction or use of this work in any form or by any electronic, mechanical or other
means now known or hereinafter invented, including photocopying and record-
ing, and in any information storage and retrieval system is forbidden without the
written permission of the publisher.

04 03 02 01 00   8 7 6 5 4

Library of Congress Catalog Card Number:
93-72149

International Standard Book Number:
1-56625-025-0

Bonus Books, Inc.
160 East Illinois Street
Chicago, Illinois 60611

Printed in the United States of America

We always wanted to say this.

This is dedicated to the ones we love,
Florine and Arlene,
and also:

to the dreamers who don't follow the beaten path;
to the realists who make things happen for us dreamers;
to the not-top-10% of the class, those of us who really do the work;
to all drivers—remember, be careful out there;
and finally, to mom, for the help, for the support.

Table of Contents

Preface

Hello, I am Chris Sutherland, and just for a short time, I'm not going to speak for my brother the attorney. Like many good things in life, *Traffic Ticket Defense* was written in large part out of frustration . . . *my* frustration.

Here's the scene.

It's February, 1991. Take a windy, hilly road in the suburban New York village of Croton-on-Hudson, put a lot of ice on it from a winter storm the previous night, watch cars slide down the hill, then (here's the best part) set up a "speed trap" at the bottom of that hill to catch the "sliders." In the finest tradition of traffic code enforcement in small town America, Croton gets the bucks and the cop gets a good laugh. Not much room here for stuff like traffic safety or preventive measures.

The officer wasn't at all interested about the ice on the hill when he wrote me the ticket. I'm sure that my joke about this being a "Candid Camera" episode didn't help either.

So I took my sliding ticket to court, prepared with weather reports, safety manuals about how to drive on ice, etc. I prepared my testimony and my cross examination of the officer. Sounds good, right?

Only problem was that I made just about every mistake that I could in trial preparation (Chapter 5 is a kind of reverse autobiography of this incident). And whatever mistakes I missed up to that point, I made sure to cover at the trial (see Chapters 6 and 7).

Needless to say, the minute they (the "judge" and the DA were golfing buddies or something) decided that my newspaper weather reports from *USA Today* and *The*

New York Times were inadmissible because they were deemed "hearsay," I knew that I was in trouble.

In short, I had a good case, but I wasn't prepared properly and I was intimidated by the legal process. I lost, and it didn't even take them very long to do it.

Enter Mark Sutherland. Had I not been the macho younger brother, I would have listened to him earlier. After all, he and his partner John Farris have tried more traffic ticket cases than anyone in the past five years. Better still, Mark is a really nice guy, he undercharges his clientele, and he's a lot smarter than his natural modesty would ever allow him to admit.

Thus, this book captures the frustration of my failure as an average citizen with the incredible competence of the nation's best traffic attorney. For me, revenge will be sweet on the day that this book shows up in a Croton courtroom tied to a "Not Guilty" verdict.

Now that I've told you why this book is, let's be real clear about what it isn't:

This is *Not* a Law Book

It does not have comprehensive case citations, supporting briefs, 50 state vehicular code lists, etc. If it did, you'd buy the book by the pound instead of the pages.

What *Traffic Ticket Defense* is is a guide to general principle and theory. In other words, it will tell you how to do it, not what to do. You must adapt these "rules of the road" to your particular circumstances and case.

If you're still a bit confused, here are a few good ways to look at it:

1. Don't say what the book says. Say things like what the book says that are relevant to your case.

2. Don't ask questions that are in the book. Ask questions that are like what is in the book that are relevant to your case. And listen to the answers.

3. Don't use the defenses that are in the book. Use defenses that are like what is in the book.

"Well then, what good are the examples if I can't use them?" you ask. Simply put, these examples are based on the successful defenses of over 1,000 tried cases. As the cook said, "We are definitely going to give you the right recipes, but, honey, you've got to do the cookin'."

Using the principles instead of the exact facts of these examples will allow you to be flexible in preparing your own defense.

Finally, learn from yet another of my mistakes. I got way too wound up in the mean cop, the surly DA and the apathetic judge. I lost perspective and therefore objectivity. If you're unsure about your own perspective, calm down, "chill out," then read Chapters 2 and 3 carefully. You might be pleasantly surprised at the rewards you will reap.

Do it right, have fun doing it, and maybe I'll see you in Croton one day.

Chapter One

HIGHWAY ROBBERY

N ot so long ago, the countryside was full of highwaymen, bands of armed thieves who preyed
upon unsuspecting travelers, robbing them of
their money and freedom. Those who were careless and
reckless probably deserved their fate. But many were
simply innocent victims of the likes of Billy the Kid and
Black Bart.

Today, a form of highway robbery lives on. It is
called "vehicular code enforcement," otherwise known
as traffic tickets, only these days the "highwaymen" who
ply this trade are appropriately called the "Highway
Patrol."

You might be reading this because you think that
you're just caught in the traffic ticket trap, but let's keep
it in perspective. Traffic safety, typically through enforcement of the laws, is basically a good thing. It tries to keep
drunks off the road, speeders from running us down, and
all those tons of rolling steel and plastic from running
into each other.

But in the past decade or so, a trend that affects how
tickets are treated has begun to emerge in law enforce-

ment. Usually we think of traffic ticket fines as a sort of financial punishment for our sins on the road. But to the justice system, they have come to represent easy money.

Here's how they want it to work. You're caught doing 50 mph in a 40 mph zone. In your mind, you did what the "Highway Patrolman" said you were doing. You're guilty, right?

Not so fast! You may not have violated the spirit of the law. The fact that you were going 50 mph in the posted 40 mph zone means you were exceeding the speed limit, but it may have been just as "safe" as going 40 mph. Guess what, the spirit of the law (safety) wasn't violated, but the "presumption" of the law was.

But the pain of the fine, although unpleasant enough, is not the real penalty for the violation of the law. If it were only the money, you could pay the ticket and just go on with life. The more severe penalty has to do with the Department of Motor Vehicles and the loss of your license (which leads to the loss of your job, which leads to your wife and/or girlfriend leaving you, which leads to depression, which leads to the drinking problem). All this because of the 50/40 ticket.

Okay, okay, maybe it's not that bad. Maybe the DMV just turns your record over to the insurance company (you know, the only company that the law says you *have* to deal with). They'll just adjust your premium to reflect a higher risk group.

Maybe that's why getting a traffic ticket ranks so high on the recall scale, right up there with Aunt Millie's funeral, Mr. Fardnick's algebra class and oral surgery.

Think about it. Getting "pulled over" is one of those infrequent moments in life when your fate is completely in the hands of a total stranger, someone who is probably not acting in your best interests. From that awful moment when you realize that the flashing lights and siren are for YOU, to the inevitable lecture as he (or she) hands you the ticket, you are virtually and technically "under arrest." You are mad, embarrassed, frustrated and late!

Being "under arrest" is a feeling that goes well beyond the notion that you just can't drive away while the cop is standing there. It is the abrupt and complete denial of your basic freedoms for (at best) five to 10 minutes (doesn't it always seem longer?). And, in the eyes of the so-called justice system, you are a criminal.

In fact, that very presumption on the part of police officers may well have led to perhaps the most significant traffic stop in the history of law enforcement, the beating of Rodney King. Forgotten in the hailstorm of media hype and civil unrest was the fact that Rodney King was originally pulled over for speeding. It is clear that the case against the officers was based largely on their preconceived attitudes about Mr. King before he was actually stopped. Whether those attitudes were motivated by racial prejudice or the simple fact that they had had such an extended chase is, I would suggest, too fine a line for us to wonder about.

But when it comes to traffic tickets, one fact that the law enforcement system would just as soon have you overlook is that, like real criminals, people cited for traffic violations have rights, too. What those rights are, and (more importantly) how you can use them, is what this book is all about. Working within the system, use the rules (that the system makes up) to your best advantage.

You might believe that you're innocent, in which case this book is an excellent tool to prepare your defense for acquittal. But even if you are guilty, this book is about some legitimate ways to try to keep the ticket from appearing on your DMV record and in your insurance agent's files. It's also about regaining control, even if just a little bit, of one part of our government that is out of control.

But win or lose, part of your goal in reading and using this book should always include feeling good about doing something right and not letting "Big Brother" push you around.

Why Do They Have to Ticket?

Although we're talking about a system that has basically gone haywire, it's important to separate the people from the process. Cops are not automatically bad people. But when it comes to traffic tickets, they are more often good people trapped in a bad system. Understanding why tickets are written will immediately help you to better defend yourself. Here are a few clues, from the obvious to the ridiculous:

1. It's the Law!

Sounds simple, right? In fact, much of this book will deal with the reality that you may indeed be guilty, and that minimizing the consequences should be your goal.

But more often than you think, it isn't THAT they enforce the law, it is HOW and WHY. Let's look a little deeper.

2. The Economics of Traffic Law Enforcement

Have you ever been to a tax hearing? Generally, if an increase is being proposed, it is not a pretty sight. Angry citizens grill embarrassed politicians and bureaucrats about already high tax rates and the next election. The notion of exploring less painful ways of finding money must be very appealing.

The Nineties, in particular, have been especially hard on government funding. In 1991, no fewer than seven states, including California and New York, posted budget deficits in excess of one billion dollars. New York alone projected losses of $3.6 billion. Add to that a stagnant economy, and the temptation to bend the systems in search of a few extra dollars becomes very attractive.

Enter the criminal justice system.

Sure, locking up murderers and rapists is important, but that costs money. By writing traffic tickets, local and state agencies are not only upholding the LAW, they are also getting money—lots of it—from people who usually don't complain about having to pay a fine. Less than 10% of those who receive a ticket will ever fight it!

The result is a one-billion-dollar windfall to government, with virtually no organized opposition. In a very real sense, traffic cops know that they are helping to protect their own salaries by writing tickets.

Whether in the cities or on the highways, the purpose of "traffic" officers is to enforce the "traffic" laws. Their function is to look for violations, and they are good at it. Their performance is based (somewhat) on the number of tickets written, and to some extent their salaries are connected to the fines collected by the courts.

Put another way, how many parking tickets would really be issued if mandatory jail terms replaced fines?

The Power of the Pen

There are very few times when a cop is more confident of his or her actions than when he or she is writing a traffic ticket. Police brutality, use of service revolver, and conflict of interest issues strike fear in the heart of every law enforcement official. But hand them a pen and a ticket book, and they all become Clint Eastwood's "Dirty" Harry Callahan. A cop never thinks he's wrong about a traffic ticket. Later, you will see how that inherent over-confidence is one of *your* best weapons.

The point is we have come to live with a traffic enforcement system that desperately needs money, started by police officers who for the most part want to write tickets. Notice that I haven't mentioned "justice" yet?

And although you won't win every time you fight a ticket, you will make them earn your money, just as you will earn their respect.

Sometimes that's enough.

Chapter Two

WHY YOU'RE READING THIS BOOK AND NOT CALLING AN ATTORNEY

This book is not just about the "injustice" system. It is about you, the traffic ticket in your hand, and what you can and should do about it. You'll learn a lot about how the traffic justice system works and about how lawyers and prosecutors work within it. You'll have a little fun and a positive court experience, and we hope you'll win, but at the very least you're going to make them earn that fine.

In Chapter 1 we saw how the consequences of a ticket go well beyond the fine that is imposed by the court and the ramifications of the DMV and the insurance company. However, these are not fatal or life-threatening conditions. It's always important to balance the worst-case scenario and how much time and money you can honestly invest with your chances of winning and feeling good about the outcome, whatever it is.

That's one reason you should not hire a lawyer for simple cases. Once you "retain" counsel, you in effect give up any commitment to your case . . . as in, "it's in my lawyer's hands now." As long as you're only dealing with a little money and/or some traffic school, a lawyer is probably going to cost you more than the ticket is worth. I know. I do this for a living.

> *WARNING: Using this book for more than what it is intended to do could be hazardous to your driving record.*

> *Before we go on, heed this warning. The vast majority of traffic violations are minor and their defense can be planned in the pages of this book. But if you are in any way unsure of what could happen to you, you must read Chapter 10. Take the "I'd Better Call Somebody" Test to see if you do need help. Felony convictions, suspended licenses, drunk driving and jail terms are nothing to fool around with, and professional help is sometimes mandatory.*

So let's assume you've passed the test in Chapter 10, and I haven't scared you off from beating the system. Here are three reasons to read on:

1. Nobody cares more about you, your case, your driving record and your wallet than you (with the possible exception of your mother).

2. This book will give you an honest chance to adequately defend your case without the need (and expense) of an attorney.

3. With the use of this book you will have some distinct advantages even over having an attorney. The greatest advantage (and sometimes the greatest disadvantage) is that you yourself know and can recall all the facts concerning your case. You are and can be a witness to the event and also be your own attorney. You'll know what to argue and how to present your case. You need not become a legal scholar to enjoy the thrill of a trial.

Follow the steps in *Traffic Ticket Defense for the Presumed Guilty* and you're going to have a little fun, gain confidence in your ability to control a situation that you thought was uncontrollable, and become better organized. And hey, you're going to give yourself the best chance to win!

Chapter Three

WHAT TO DO WHEN YOU'RE STOPPED

B eg, plead, whine. You have nothing to lose except your dignity, and dignity doesn't go on your driving record!

You see the flashing red light go on behind you and a sinking feeling comes over you. Ideally, you're alone, so you avoid snickers or lectures from inside the car.

But be careful. The cop, at this time, is as afraid of you as you are of him, and he is watching every move you make. From the cop's point of view, it's one of the most dangerous parts of his routine. Remain calm, place both hands on the wheel and wait for him to approach you. You're probably mad as hell right now, but this is not the time to do anything about it.

> DO NOT reach for your wallet under the seat or reach towards the glove compartment. This is a simple traffic violation. Keep it that way.

> DO NOT unbuckle your seat belt or pretend that you are unbuckling your seat belt if you're not wearing one.

> DO NOT do anything to make him any more suspicious of you than he already is. Remember, it may only be a

traffic ticket to you, but *he* doesn't know whether or not his life is at stake for those few seconds.

Whatever side of the issue you're on, there is little doubt that Rodney King wishes he had handled his "routine" speeding ticket differently.

Once formal introductions are exchanged, i.e. your license and registration, and the officer realizes that you're not a homicidal maniac, it is now social time. The cop's job is usually boring and monotonous and his only chance to talk to people is at stops like yours. Be polite, kind, courteous, reverent and brave (isn't that the Scout's motto?), but DON'T ADMIT YOUR GUILT.

This is the time to try to "talk" your way out of it. Tell him about your sick aunt who needs open-heart surgery, your lousy boss, or your tough day. Better still, get him to talk about *his* aunt/boss/day. DO NOT tell him anything about your driving. Remember, whine, beg, plead, but don't discuss the facts of your case.

If the infraction was minor, the officer may let you off with a warning. Cops have a heart (ha!) sometimes. You may be able to talk your way out of this ticket. If he thinks you are a pleasant sort, he may give you a break or reduce the charge or lower the speed of your vehicle. Right now he is determining what the *facts* are and how many violations there will be. Also, he will be less likely to remember you if you give him nothing unusual to jog his memory at the trial. Keep it low key. The one thing to keep in the glove compartment is your ego . . . you want to be forgettable.

On the other hand, his job is to write tickets. He has already stopped you, so there's a pretty good chance he's going to write a ticket no matter what. Sometimes, you may not be able to talk your way out of a ticket. But "cop an attitude," and you can sure as hell talk your way into one (and maybe more).

Street Lesson Number 1:

Here's a problem I have with a client about once a month. We'll call him "Mike".

The cop was going to warn Mike (it seems as if almost all the "attitude" tickets are men) about a taillight out. Not giving the cop a chance to say that, Mike got upset and started arguing about how the traffic light was really yellow and how the cop was too far away from the intersection to see. Not content with calling the cop an incompetent jerk, Mike then reminds the officer just who pays the cop's salary, and that Mike's best friend's brother knows someone on the City Council. Not only did Mike just talk his way into probably several new offences, Mike will be very lucky if that's all he's facing.

Here's the hard part. Everything Mike said may have been absolutely true, but the street isn't the time or place to threaten or debate. His big mouth got him in a lot more trouble than he was actually stopped for, and he made the second mistake of trying to try his case on the street.

Street Lesson Number 2:

AS SOON AS THE COP'S PEN HITS THE TICKET BOOK, HE MUST WRITE THAT TICKET.

That is your cue to shut up. Do not admit anything.

This is stage one of your fact-gathering mission. Rather than trying to tell him your side of the story, find out his side. Where was he sitting when he first saw you? DON'T argue or disagree with him on any fact; save it for later. If he has radar, have him show it to you. Don't argue or admit, just take notes. While you're silently preparing your defense, you want to maintain a low profile so that he doesn't remember you. This will help you in court.

Remember, stopping you is no big deal to him. He knows that most of his tickets aren't going to trial and you're just one of many. Use this to your advantage; remain calm, don't admit anything. Resist the urge to try your case out in the street. No matter how much you want to, don't let him know you're planning to fight the ticket.

Here are some tips on channeling your anger. Ask the cop questions about his car, how long he's been on duty, if it's been a tough day. Pump him for information. He will be doing the same thing to you, in addition to trying to get you to admit guilt.

If things get a little heated, remember that this is the U.S.A. and you DO have a constitutional right to remain silent. If he persists, ask him if you can refuse to answer any of his questions, knowing you can. Politely tell him you would rather not discuss the case with him.

Street Lesson Number 3:

> *You have the right to remain silent, but in traffic cases, the cop doesn't have to advise ("Mirandize") you of it!*

Street Lesson Number 4:

The instinct of most people is to answer the questions asked by the officer, but these are usually dumb answers to even dumber questions. Here's just a sample of five tricks that they will try to pull on you, along with some "before-his-pen-hits-the-pad" answers:

Cop's General Purpose: To get you to admit guilt.

Question 1.   Do you know why I stopped you?

Answer.   No, Officer, I honestly don't.

Q 2.   Do you know how fast you were going?

A.   The speed limit, I think.
Faster than the minimum speed limit?

Q 3.   Did you see that light back there?

A.   Do you mean the green one?
Which one, Officer?

Q 4.   Did you have your seat belt on?

A.   Yes (three weeks ago).

Q 5.   Did you know your license was suspended?

A.   No (if you REALLY don't know or can't remember).
Do I have to answer that?

Obviously, the line between deflecting humor and nasty sarcasm can be very thin, especially when you're angry and he's a jerk (they're allowed, you know). The idea of these kinds of answers is to change the normal cop/criminal routine into two nice people just doin' their jobs.

Let's say you still get a ticket. The cop may be taking notes after he gives you the ticket. You do the same. Keep quiet and start your own investigation.

Details are important, so gather as many facts as you can. At the trial you may want to divert the cop's attention away from the violation and onto the details, especially if he is not as sure of his facts as you are of yours. You will remember the major issues, such as the color of the light or your speed. However, the "facts" that may slip your memory are those that will not appear on the face of the ticket. Here are some typical checks for you to make:

1. The exact location where he stopped you.

2. The distance between where the violation occurred and where you were stopped.

3. The color of your shirt.

4. Who said what to whom.

5. Passengers or other witnesses.

6. Some distinctive thing about your car (e.g., mag wheels, roll bars, fog lights, a big dent).

7. The weather (other than what's on the ticket).

8. His actions (for example, did he do something unusual that he may forget later?).

It will be important to ask questions about details like these. These will be important at the time of trial. The more details you can put down at the time of the incident, the more accurate your testimony, and the less accurate the officer's will seem.

The idea here is to establish "reasonable doubt" by testing the officer's memory at trial. The smaller the detail, the better (e.g., "It says here, officer, that you noticed a faulty front turn signal, yet you can't seem to remember whether or not the car had fog lights?").

To be sure of your facts, take your notes at or near the time of the stop. You can be sure that the cop is making notes on the back of his copy. *But your notes will be better because you care more about your ticket than he does.* When the testimony comes down to your word against his, the judge should take into consideration the ability to recall the events as one test of credibility. That's why making these notes and diagrams is really crucial. Do it right then and there!

Next, make a detailed diagram of the area. Include distances between points by the use of a best-guess method or the odometer on your car. Be as accurate as possible, then strengthen the diagram by adding bushes, trees, walls, buildings, width of lanes, and downgrades or upgrades. Also add traffic control devices and signs, and include their placement (e.g., where were the last speed limit sign and next speed limit sign?).

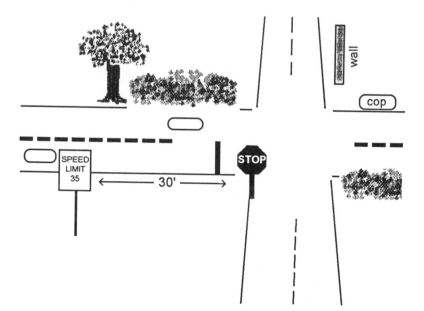

Note any confusing or conflicting signs, as well as the size and location of all signs and any obstructions of them. I once heard that a New York City ticket was dismissed because it was proven that the motorist had to read, comprehend and react to 46 different signs or traffic control devices at the same intersection.

Some of these physical facts may be detrimental to your case, but be accurate about the physical aspect because the judge may go take a look or know the location. It may hurt your case if you misrepresent the situation. If the physical facts themselves hurt your case, then you can choose not to use pictures or diagrams for your side of the case at trial.

The more important areas in the investigation are the transient or moving "facts". These are the elements that change, such as speed, the color of the light, the length of time for the red, green or yellow phasing of the light, traffic conditions and what was said. These moments in time will be lost forever if you don't note them accurately as soon as you can after they happen! Your memory will only fade with time, so make the notes right away.

These are the conditions that are subject to interpretation by you and the officer. Note them down. Make them as accurate as possible to support witness credibility at the time of trial. The fact that you were in the fast lane and a car passed you in the slow lane as you went through the yellow light may be of significance at trial. Even insignificant facts may be important to establish recall at the time of trial.

Here are some practical examples:

Note the traffic around you: what kind, what color, what position (ahead, behind). This observation on your part could be relevant especially if other traffic could have confused the officer, causing him to pick out the wrong car.

If you were caught in a speed trap, the use of radar may have been affected by large trucks or cars traveling in the opposite direction, or a larger vehicle behind you, or high power lines, or transmitters in the area.

Go back and check the phasing of the light, how long it stays red/yellow/green, and see if the cop comes back to the location of the light after he releases you. In a red light situation, the cop will usually testify that he went back to the location and noted that the signal was functioning properly. This may be a lie, but if you didn't go back, there will be no evidence to refute that testimony. Go back and hang out (preferably with a friend as a witness) for a few minutes and see if he does come back.

This may seem like a lot of effort, but it will pay off at trial when you are questioning the officer. Even if the question has no relevance to the citation, you may be asking enough questions to raise a reasonable doubt as to the officer's observations. Better still, a very common but rarely exploited weakness is the officer's independent present recollection at the time of trial. Under the 6th Amendment to the Constitution, you have a right to confront and cross-examine the witness against you. If the cop can't remember ("No independent recollection"), then you have been denied that right.

Questions concerning the physical description of the location of your citation are great for establishing "reasonable doubt." Here is a perfect "no lose" example:

Q. Officer, please describe the scene where you observed this alleged violation.

Once you get in court, here are some possible answers:

1. The cop accurately describes the location. **Good!** Just go on to the next thing.

2. The cop takes a "Nixon" defense, i.e., "I don't recall at this time." **Better!** Later, you can say that the cop has insufficient recollection of the events. The more "I don't know" responses you can elicit from him, the stronger your argument will be for no present recollection.

3. The cop lies regarding the physical description. **Best!** This is the perfect response for your case. You will

have positive evidence that the cop has "lied" under oath.

But be careful here. Answers 2 and especially 3 may give you the upper hand at this point, but you haven't won the case yet. Even if he lied, jumping too fast on nailing the cop in the lie might tip your hand that you're on to him too soon. Your time can wait until you've allowed him to completely botch his testimony. Just stop and take clear notes of his error.

Now do you see how getting all those details will help your case? It will allow you to ask pointed questions at trial that will lead to a conclusion of reasonable doubt, and ultimately, "Not Guilty!"

Let's go back to the scene. While you are waiting for the officer to complete your ticket, try to make a mental video of the incident. Rather than trying to remember isolated facts, get a good mental image in your head, then stop and recall individual facts.

Here comes what may be the hardest part. By this time, you're probably angry, frustrated and (if you've read this book) anxious to nail this guy. Don't! Your time will come, but it is *not* now.

After the cop hands you the ticket, sign it, and make no parting comments about seeing him in court. *It is to your advantage to be completely forgettable to that cop.* Look at your copy of the ticket and go through it line by line. Start with the date and time, name, make and model. Check for accuracy, but DO NOT bring any problems to the attention of the police officer. The ticket has already been issued, and you don't want to correct the officer until you have him in court. You will use the inaccuracy to attack his credibility at the trial. Look for the violation section and check the place of incident, speed, etc. It is here that you might find errors committed by the officer that could mean instant acquittal.

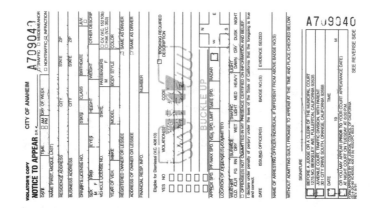

For example, an error in code section or location may win your case. Use the "Archie Bunker" maneuver and "stifle yourself." Calling the cop a jerk and pointing out the mistake will:

1. Embarrass and maybe tick him off (that's something you want to happen in court, *not* on the street).

2. Give him a chance to fix the mistake (then deny it in court).

3. Make you the mental highlight of his day.

Remember, every cop begins with the idea that you are guilty, so you must find holes in his case. The best way to do that is to not let him know that you're looking.

Finally, you may have more legitimate cards to play. Note where the time and place is for your appearance. Some states allow you to change the place of your appearance by requesting that the police officer at the scene have the case transferred to the county seat.

In a polite but clear tone, ASK THE OFFICER TO CHANGE THE APPEARANCE TO THE COUNTY SEAT.

Don't argue with the cop if he refuses, but have him note it on the citation that you requested it. Again, be polite and courteous, but DON'T ADMIT TO ANYTHING.

Finally, after receiving the ticket, most people are angry and want to rip it up and throw it away. Don't! Put it in a safe place. This ticket, like it or not, is your evidence. The police officer can't change anything on the face of the ticket without notifying you in writing of the change. You can check this at the time of the trial for any changes . . . unless you threw the ticket away or mangled it beyond recognition.

The citation will also have the time and place for your court appearance. This is the only legal notice the government is required to give you. When you sign the ticket you are promising to appear on or before the date stated. They do not need to send a "courtesy notice" or "reminder" to you.

Also, in spite of how you feel, don't be too quick to drive away. Look at where you are. Casually notice what the cop is doing. Is he:

- Finishing his donut? Good! You're becoming forgettable already.

- Writing on your ticket and making notes? Not so good. He may just be a good cop doing a thorough job, or you may have tipped him off that you are going to fight this ticket.

- On the radio running a warrant or license check? Short of arrest, the worst! You definitely did something to arouse his suspicions. If he's letting you go at this point, then go.

This may give you an indication of how seriously he is taking the job. But again, you are now conducting your own investigation, so don't wait around too long. You might even pull away and make your observation from some other location (e.g., get some gas at the station on the corner in front of you).

If you have the time and the energy, go back and retrace your exact route. This time you'll be looking for details and distances:

- See where the cop was positioned and what he could (or couldn't) observe.

- Make note of possible lighting obstructions or other impediments to his judgment. A Long Island man once contested a "No Left Turn" ticket because he observed that the sign that was cited in the ticket was 17 feet off the ground. New York State says it can't be any more than 8 feet. Guess what? In court, he made the correct citation of law, but forgot to note the proper date on the copy of the code he was quoting from. The judge acknowledged the law, but pronounced him "Guilty." The next day the sign was changed to 8 feet.

- Make simple diagrams of the area.

Make notes to yourself at this time, or as soon as is practical afterward. You may think that you'll never forget what that jerk said to you—or what kind of car had cut you off, or whatever is burned into your mind at that moment. But if you don't make notes, time will fade the best of memories. With the additional pressure of a court trial, you may inadvertently forget a crucial bit of information.

Okay, the ticket's been issued, and you've made your notes. Now forget about it, go on with life, and enjoy the rest of the day. If you relax, you'll probably think about the incident from time to time, remembering additional details. Write them down. Think about and analyze the situation not just from your own perspective, but from the police officer's, too. You may come up with something.

But remember, letting him enjoy the rest of his do-nut is the quickest way for you to become a blur in his memory, and a cop's blurring memory is your ally.

Chapter Four

WHAT TO DO ABOUT YOUR TICKET

When the police officer's pen hits the ticket book—you lose. No matter what, time and money are taken away from you. Add to that some secondary consequences not directly apparent, like DMV points and insurance rates, and it becomes obvious why you must at least consider all the alternatives in order to minimize your losses.

But before we discuss those alternatives, you must evaluate your own set of criteria, also known as a "gut check."

Several days after the ticket (but before your arraignment date) is the best time to seriously consider your options. You want the waiting period to help you calm down so that you can make the best decision for yourself.

The key here is to keep the objective in line. What do you want to see happen? Take this quick test to assess your true purposes in going forward:

I want to fight this ticket because (check all that apply):

_____ I want to prevent it from going on my record.

_____ I can't afford the fine.

_____ It's not fair! I didn't do it.

_____ It's not fair! I did it, but so did everybody else.

_____ I can't afford the points on my license.

_____ I'm embarrassed, and fighting the ticket makes me feel better.

_____ The cop was a jerk and I want to embarrass him.

_____ None of the above, but I know ('cause I read this book) that the cop screwed up and I can get off. I want to allow the system to lose its case.

While some of these reasons are probably more valid than others, none are "wrong" answers. However, all of them require you to evaluate your options and analyze the consequences of the situation. For example, you always drive this fast but you've been lucky that you haven't been caught more often. Or, this is your first ticket in 23 years of driving, and this will never happen again.

One final point that must override all others is a personal one: Risk Tolerance. It doesn't matter how strong your case is, or how well you've come to understand the process. If you are the kind of person who hates confrontation, especially with the "system," think twice before you proceed. Nobody likes to be told that they messed up, and that's essentially what you'll be telling policemen and even judges (or at least that's how they may well take it).

Whatever your reasons for considering alternatives, your choices are really quite simple:

(1) TRAFFIC SCHOOL

(2) GUILTY

(3) NOT GUILTY

You have to be ready to pick one of these before your arraignment date. Let's look at them in detail.

Option 1: Go to School

If money is an issue, traffic school may be a good and cheaper option. Most states have a Driver Safety Class that minor violators can attend. The court will dismiss the case and the Department of Motor Vehicles (DMV) will not use the citation as a point count, nor will they release the information to the public (i.e. insurance companies and your place of employment). If you're facing a loss of your license because of this ticket, traffic school is an excellent option to consider. The single clear advantage of traffic school is that it offers guaranteed dismissal.

In some cases, the chance of going to trial and losing is too great to justify the risk. For example, if this is the one and only ticket of your life, then keeping your perfect record might well mean traffic school.

However, if you're like a lot of us, you may want to save the traffic school option for when you REALLY need it. Most insurance companies will not raise your rates for one citation on your record. But for two or more there may be a significant increase. Before you decide on this option you may want to call your insurance company and ask about their policy.

You want to optimize your opportunity for the use of traffic school. If one ticket will not affect your rates, you may want to take a chance on your first ticket and take it to trial. If you win, you won't have any points on your record, and you'll have saved the traffic school option for a later date. If you lose your first trial, then traffic school is always there for you on the next ticket. You want to minimize the chances of getting two points on your record.

Sometimes you want to avail yourself of traffic school and the clerk or the court refuses to grant you that option. Keep asking at each level; ask the clerk, ask at the arraignment and ask at court before and after the trial. They only have to say "Yes" once.

Also, there may be a second level of traffic school or a Commercial Driver Traffic School available in the county you're in. Keep asking, and if traffic school is your choice, keep trying to get it.

There are some disadvantages to traffic school. For one thing, it is more expensive than the original ticket (in California it's the full amount of the fine plus between $24 and $48 additional). It's also eight hours (or so) of your time, sitting in a classroom while your favorite team is on TV or while there's something else you'd rather be doing.

Option 2: Pay Up

Nine out of 10 people just pay the ticket. They figure that since they were guilty (they did what the officer said they did), they should just admit guilt and not contest the citation.

The advantage of "paying up" is that this usually can be done with the aid of the Postal Service. Send a check (or money order) with the citation and that's the end of it.

Remember Chapter 1? The legal system loves this kind of thinking, but you should hate it! After the cop's pen hits the pad, you have nothing to lose by fighting your ticket.

> *WHETHER YOU PLEAD GUILTY AND PAY THE FINE (BAIL FORFEITURE) OR ARE FOUND GUILTY IN COURT, THE CONSEQUENCES ARE THE SAME.*

The points go on your record, your insurance rates may go up, and your employer will have access to the record. If traffic school is not an option, then you might as well take a chance and exercise your right to a trial.

It's really this simple. There are only three reasons to plead guilty:

- Time

- Distance

- Paranoia

While we're on the subject of fear, let's cover an option that is no option at all: *ignoring the citation.* No kidding around, this is just plain dumb!

For starters, ignoring the citation will result in a warrant for your arrest issued for Failure To Appear (FTA). With a seemingly innocent oversight, you will have transformed a rather insignificant traffic ticket infraction into a misdemeanor for which you could be placed in jail. Not worth it.

How dumb is this, you ask? Let's just glance at the snowball effects of having a warrant out for your arrest. How about wrecking a wonderful Saturday night date as you're hauled off to jail because you had a taillight out and the cop ran a check on your license and found the FTA. Hope you have cab fare home for your date.

A little closer to home, what is more serious is that the court notifies the DMV, who in turn suspends your license. Now the next time you are stopped, you are driving on a suspended license. This is as serious (in California) as a Driving Under the Influence (DUI) charge.

But wait, there's more! Most of the states are now inter-connected with the aid of computers. So if you get a ticket in Texas, it will show up on your California DMV report. Consequently, if you get a Failure to Appear in California, your Rhode Island license will not be reissued until the citation is cleared.

Get the picture? DEAL WITH THE TICKET BEFORE IT DEALS WITH YOU! You may want to write the court for an extension or "trial by declaration," but deal with it NOW.

So, let's say you're going to deal with it, but traffic school is not an option and the idea of just paying it makes you throw up (or whatever). Let's look at your final option.

Option 3: The "No Lose" Approach

Let's get one thing straight from the start.

A NOT GUILTY plea, legally, doesn't mean you didn't do it. NOT GUILTY, legally, means the prosecution hasn't proven you guilty beyond a reasonable doubt. The prosecution has the burden of proof, *not you.* The fact that the court has a citation stating that you were doing 70 mph in a 55 mph zone does not alone have any evidenciary (the stuff that makes you guilty) weight against you. In reality the court will attempt to presume you guilty, even though the law states that you are presumed innocent.

You may not like the idea of a trial, but if you look at the alternatives, this may be the only viable decision for you. Here's a possible scenario:

1. Traffic school may be an option, but you work on the nights that it's offered. It will cost you more in lost wages than the ticket and higher insurance combined.

2. The court's preference, pleading guilty and paying the fine, is always there. But because all the negative consequences will occur without even the *chance* of winning the case, why not go for it?

So, although the NOT GUILTY COURT TRIAL option is not your favorite, it is very often the "best" decision.

Once you've decided to "go for it," you may or may not want to become an investigator or an attorney in order to fight your ticket. Since no one is going to jail here, you're in a "no lose" situation. Having a trial is better than not having one. Being prepared is even better. Keep this in perspective and have a little fun along the way. Remember, what you learn in your preparation can even have beneficial effects in other areas of your life.

> *Speaking of "going to jail," here's an important perspective to keep in mind. You may not get thrown in jail for the traffic ticket that you're fighting, but you can for "Contempt of Court." Walk into court with a major attitude and start insulting the judge because he doesn't see it your way, then watch how fast a simple little traffic court trial can turn into a major problem. While traffic court may not be for the meek, it is definitely not for somebody who simply can't control his or her temper.*

Back to your preparation. You can have a full blown trial with photos, diagrams and all the "legal eagle" stuff, or simply a "trial by declaration," which is nothing more than a written statement presented to the court without the need for a personal appearance.

Fighting the ticket can be a very wise decision. A court trial can be exciting and entertaining. You no longer want to think in terms of being guilty, but in terms of how the prosecution has failed to support the allegations against you, thus allowing you to win.

You are more in control of this process than you think!

A final point on decision making here: Don't struggle with trying to make the "right" decision. Spend your analytical and emotional energy trying to make the "best" decision. Going to trial may not be your first choice, but it is a good choice when you consider the alternatives. You should make the decision that is right for you.

And once you decide, then DECIDE! Be emphatic and enthusiastic about what you're doing. By "attacking" your decision, you become a winner no matter what the outcome of the case.

Chapter Five

FROM CURBSIDE TO COURTSIDE

Y ou'll have approximately one month between the time you get the ticket and your arraignment date. Once you've decided to consider fighting the ticket, this should be one of your productive times.

First, collect the necessary information to help you make that decision.

- Call your insurance agent to see what ramifications a ticket would have on your rates.

- Contact the DMV to see what your record looks like and what the consequences of a new ticket would be.

- Find out when you last went to traffic school and see if you are eligible to go again.

- Check out your upcoming school or work schedule in case you opt for traffic court.

- If you have paperwork to get done, such as registering your car, get it done now before arraignment, so it will be handled before trial.

- If you have a "fix-it" ticket, get it FIXED and signed off by the appropriate authorities.

A common mistake occurs when a person gets a "fix-it" ticket (headlight out) and the cop tells him that if he gets it fixed and signed off, the ticket will be dismissed. So the person gets it fixed, has the ticket signed off and THINKS it is dismissed because that's what the cop told him. That isn't correct, because you have to get the signed-off "fix-it" ticket to court *for the court to dismiss the ticket.* If you don't do so before the date of your court appearance (at the bottom of the ticket), a "Failure to Appear" (FTA) will be added. Again, you will have transformed a ticket that would cost you little or nothing into a misdemeanor. Take care of "fix-it" tickets, and get them to court before your due date.

• Depending on time, energy and money, you may want to review your case with an attorney to see if there are any legal defenses available to you.

• You may want to go to court to familiarize yourself with the procedure. It'll make you feel more comfortable when you need to do it yourself. You may want to visit your local law library and just look at what you're actually charged with.

Keep in mind, these points are not a checklist that will give you the "right" answer. In fact, you don't have to do any of this to reach a decision. It is your ticket, your record, but most importantly, your peace of mind!

About the Court

The court is an intimidating place, cloaked in an atmosphere of autonomous mystery. It seems like people don't work there, just systems and procedures. Guess what? This is done on purpose. Courts try to:

1) Be as cold as possible. They are busy and want to handle as many cases as quickly as possible.

2) Be efficient to the point of rudeness and intimidation. The Court is there to inform you of your Rights. But since they know what the Rights are, they usually try to inform you quickly and in as much of a monotone as possible. It's important that *you* understand the Rights (not that the Court does).

3) The Court needs to get a plea from you. (Now, without ever saying so, the Court wants you to plead GUILTY.)

Arraignment

The bottom of your ticket states a time and place for your appearance. That date is actually your arraignment date. There will be no trial and no police officer there. This is simply a process in which you will be notified of your rights and, as you learned in the last chapter, you will enter one of these pleas:

1) Guilty, no trial and pay a fine (yeech!).

2) Traffic School, then go to school.

3) Not Guilty, trial at a later date.

Virtually all traffic court arraignments are handled in one of three ways:

1) The clerk at the window may handle the entire procedure. That is, you can hand the clerk the citation and he or she will give you a date to appear for trial.

2) Sometimes, you must go before a judge to personally enter a "Not Guilty" plea and request a court trial.

3) Some courts allow you to request a court trial by mail. You mail in a copy of the citation and request a date for trial. While this is the most convenient alternative, it's important that you send a copy, NOT the original (whether a copy is requested or not). Remember what we said about discrepancies!

Pick a date convenient to your schedule. You may not get it, but the worst the court can say is "No."

A Matter of Bail

Some courts will require you to "post bail", which means put up the amount of the fine to ensure your appearance in court on the date of trial. Then if you're found Guilty, they will apply the bail towards your fine. If you're found Not Guilty, it will usually take six to eight weeks for the court to return it to you. This sounds like a pre-payment penalty, or, at best, a two- to three-month loan to the state. You will lose the use of the money for that time, but there are advantages:

1) When you do go to trial you will really have nothing to lose because your ante is already up in the form of the bail.

2) If for some reason you're unable to make the court trial date, the bail will be forfeited, and (in most cases) there are no further proceedings.

If you don't post the bail and then fail to appear, a Bench Warrant will go out for you and you will be subject to arrest.

Sure, it's painful to part with the money to the court, but it may be required, or at least in your best interest to do so.

About Your Rights

Why does it always sound like when cops, court clerks and judges say you have "rights," they are doing you a Great Favor? Just remind yourself, it's all part of the **Great Intimidation Game**.

Even if this is a parking ticket, those rights are guaranteed. A murderer, rapist or burglar has no more right to those rights than you do. So don't feel like you're imposing on the system's time and resources. Give those rights up (Waiver of Rights), and you, in fact, are giving the court a "break."

Just like the most serious felon, you, too, have "Defendant's Rights." You have to know of those rights and use them to your benefit. The government is making the rules, you're just playing by them; use them to your advantage.

Let's look at a few of your rights:

1) Right to a speedy trial

2) Right to a court trial

3) Right to confront and cross-examine witnesses

4) Right to subpoena witnesses

5) Right to an attorney

6) Right to remain silent

Here are the details:

1) **You have a right to a speedy trial**. Usually that means that the Prosecution has 45 days from the date of your arraignment to get you to trial. That is a "drop dead" date for the state. If they don't get you to trial within the 45 days, the case (with few exceptions) will be dismissed. As with most laws, there are al-

ways exceptions to the rules; so it is with the right to a speedy trial. The state may have valid reasons to extend the case beyond the 45 days, but they will have to justify them.

At arraignment the court may ask you if you waive (give up) the right to a speedy trial. If you do, then the court can set your trial date beyond the 45 days for your convenience (that's good), or for the convenience of the prosecution (that's bad). Just know that if you waive your right, you can't change your mind later.

There are disadvantages to standing on your speedy trial right:

a) The court can give you any date within the 45 day period (usually 30 to 35 days from the arraignment) that may be inconvenient to your schedule.

b) The ticket may be still fresh in the cop's memory, which may hurt your case.

c) You may feel additional pressure of time to prepare your case. *Warning to Procrastinators!* Do not delay your case so you don't have to deal with it. You're not going to be any better prepared in two months than you will be 45 days down the road. Your facts won't be any better nor the law any stronger with a "Time Waiver." Resist the urge to waive time. (You ain't going to get any smarter.)

d) You give up the time clock if you waive time to the prosecution. Now they can pick the date they want.

Conversely, there are a few advantages to waiving time. The most important is the fact that the more time between the incident and the trial, the less likely the cop will remember the facts of the case. So, if you can get a year-and-a-half continuance, go for it. (The court will only give a month or two.) Usually the advantage does not outweigh the disadvantage.

2) **You have a right to a Court Trial.** While you always have the right to a court trial, that usually means that a judge is also acting as the jury. If they do tell you that you have a right to a jury trial, it could be a warning sign that you may need an attorney (you will now have a right to an appointed attorney). In other words, a jury trial could mean a lot more trouble than you thought, so don't mess around with this yourself. Get help.

    In either case, the court trial will be held *only* if you request it. So, REQUEST IT!

3) **You have a right to an attorney.** You can hire your own attorney at any stage of the proceedings at your own expense. Unlike most criminal cases, the court DOES NOT have to appoint you an attorney, even if you would qualify for one. If you do choose an attorney, you can't wait until the day of the trial to get one. The attorney won't be ready and the court is unlikely to grant a continuance.

    But be careful. The first job of any attorney is to get your money. Sure, attorneys may know more court procedure or rules of evidence than you, but 1) they weren't there when you got the ticket, and 2) this isn't a big case for them.

    The point is that you're likely to do as good a job as an attorney in this matter.

    Having tried to ease your mind about being your own attorney, be sure to refer to Chapter 10. There are times to call in the hired guns, so don't assume too much.

For example, an attorney may assist you in the preparation of your case, or may appear for you WITHOUT THE NEED FOR YOU TO GO TO COURT. They can also lower the anxiety at trial and be more objective in cross-examining the officer.

Keep even this possibility in perspective. Attorneys are not miracle workers, they generally cost too much, and they can offer no guarantee of acquittal.

4) **You have a right to confront and cross-examine witnesses against you.** As long as you don't give up the right by pleading GUILTY or opting for traffic school, that means the cop has to come to court and testify. At best, he won't show, and you win the case; at the very least, you'll irritate and inconvenience the cop (really neat if that was one of your goals. After all, he did it to you). It is important to realize that this principle applies to all allegations, even parking tickets. The cop must be present and testify, and you have the right to ask questions.

5) **You have the right to subpoena witnesses or documents on your behalf.** This means you can get court orders for documents to be served compelling other persons or documents to be in court on the date of your trial. This is your right, but be careful not to use it to your detriment.

For example, you might want to subpoena the two cops who were in the car, and it would be nice to have the two cops trying to recount the "same" story (but you'll always get inconsistencies between two people seeing the same thing). HOWEVER, you don't really want that other cop there if he'll hurt your case; also if the first cop doesn't show up, then the state may prove the case against you with the second cop.

In short, subpoenas are a great tool, but like all tools, they must be used wisely.

You also have the right to subpoena documents on your behalf, such as speed surveys from the city, showing the normal speeds of cars for the section of road. This could be your own mechanic's records showing the results of your speedometer calibration check, or the latest calibration test on the cop's radar gun.

If you need subpoenas, use the power of the court to issue them. However, do not over-use or abuse this right. If you subpoena something that has little or no relevance to the case, you not only will hurt your case, you will also risk expanding the court's interest in you beyond just the traffic ticket. And at the time of sentencing, it may mean a higher fine.

6) **You have the right to remain silent.** This may be your most important right. Use it wisely. We'll talk more about it in the trial section.

Chapter Six

TRIAL PREPARATION

You've made all the right decisions so far. You've done your arraignment and have gotten a trial date. Now comes the work—TRIAL PREPARATION.

You may not want to become an investigator or an attorney to fight your own ticket . . . or you may.

Trial Preparation

Good Trial Preparation Will . . .

1) Give you a chance of winning

2) Lower anxiety

3) Build confidence

4) Make the trial more fun

There are different levels of preparation for trial, and since no one is going to jail here, you're in a no-lose situation. Having a trial is better than not having one;

being prepared for trial is even better. Keep this in per-spective and have a little fun.

You can have a full blown trial with photographs, diagrams and all the legal garbage, or a simple trial by declaration, which is nothing more than a written state-ment by you presented to the court without the need for you to appear.

How do you prepare? As you will see later, one of the best ways to approach any legal problem is to start at the end and work backwards. In the case of preparation, that may mean looking at the law first before going to collect the facts.

Prepare file folders for each of the following cate-gories: Legal, Physical Evidence, Testimony.

First folder: LEGAL

The cop has given you your starting point for your research. The code section for which he/she has cited you will be right on the ticket itself; for example, in the middle of the citation it will say, "22350VC Unsafe speed 50/25". You want to head for your local law library and look up Vehicle Code Section 22350 in an *"Annotated Code"* reference book. This will, in the subsection, lead you to Case Law. There may be hundreds of cases cited or just a few, but they'll look like this:

People v. Goulet 13CA4th Supp1

Now go get volume 13 of California Appelate Fourth Series and look at supplement page 1. There you will find People v. Goulet and the case will concern a speeding violation. Not all cases will support your posi-tion, so do as we "experts" do and find one that does. Briefly read it over and then copy it, putting it in the Legal Folder. Then get another case, look it up, and if it sup-ports your Not Guilty desired result, read it briefly, copy it, and put it in the folder. Do this for all the relevant cases or until you get bored or until your copying money runs out. Don't be too concerned about organization or where it will fit in your big plan.

Now go back to the original statute—22350 VC unsafe speed—and break it down line by line and phrase by phrase. This is important because the prosecution must prove EACH element against you, therefore, if they miss or omit one of the elements you win, so be careful in writing down each element. 22350VC reads:

Basic Speed Law
22350

1) *No person* (they have to I.D. you as the driver)

2) *shall drive a vehicle* (the cop or other witness has to see you driving)

3) *upon a highway* (this is given broad interpretation)

4) *at a speed greater than is reasonable or prudent* (this is the guts of the statute . . . what is reasonable or prudent)

   a) *having due regard for weather, visibility, the traffic on, and the surface and width of, the highway* (these are external factors which may work for or against you)

   b) *and in no event at a speed which endangers the safety of person or property.* (Did you endanger person or property?)

The four elements of 22350VC must be proven by the state. You'll need this list right beside you at trial. Although only one of the elements has to do with speed, you have four chances of winning. Now look back over your research and you'll see that the cases will fall into one of the 4 elements of the statute. Put it in the folder.

Second Folder: PHYSICAL EVIDENCE

Next you want to get the facts. Remember, way back when you got the ticket, you made a sketch of the area and notes. Now's the time to pull them out (don't have them? . . . not to worry). Go back to the scene of the incident and make a good diagram of the area, being as accurate as possible. Take pictures at the scene from different perspectives. Get out in the middle of the road (being careful, of course), or shoot from the driver's perspective inside the car, or from the cop's viewpoint at the donut shop. An alternative to doing this yourself is to find out whether the city has drawings or aerial shots of the intersection or roadway that could be purchased from the city engineering office. If they do you'll be getting an impartial and accurate diagram of the area.

Collect all this stuff and bring it back home. This is your "facts" folder. Prepare it for Court by either blowing up the diagram so everyone can see it in the courtroom or making enough copies so you can hand one to the Judge and Prosecution. Get the pictures developed. It is better to go for quality rather than quantity. Pick out two or three of the most relevant pictures and blow them up to 8 x 10 prints—this is more impressive to the Court than 10 shots of the same intersection. As with any evidence, you want stuff that will help your case, not hurt it. If the pictures or diagrams don't help, lose them. It is not your job to assist the prosecution in convicting you. If they choose, they can go get the photographs themselves. Put all the diagrams and/or pictures in a separate folder. Don't show them to the prosecution or police officer before trial.

Third folder: TESTIMONY

You have all those good notes you took at the scene written down. Now is the time to formalize them into a narrative of the sequence of events of that day. Be as detailed as possible. You'll have time to think of the little things now, but under the pressure of trial you may not. This should *not* be a speech you try to memorize. This is only a detailed outline of a sequence of events.

Next, get a witness statement from a friendly witness (your passenger or friend). Have him or her recall the events in his or her own words while you take notes. Help him along in crucial areas of his testimony with leading questions such as, "You remember the white Toyota in the slow lane when it passed us, right?" Have him give his answer back to you in a positive response restating your question. This will help him actually remember the incident. If he says no to the question, try to jog his memory with other related facts. If he still doesn't remember, let it go; don't tell him to say something he doesn't actually recall. At the end of the questioning, ask him if you have forgotten to ask him anything. You may be surprised at the answer. He may recall a significant fact that you forgot or he may remember something very damaging to your case. Either way, *now* is the time to be surprised by the statement, not at the time of the trial. Also, ask him some cross-examining questions to see how he does. After he's gone, evaluate his testimony: Will he help your case or not? Again, your job isn't to help the prosecution convict you.

Neutral or independent witnesses can be your best asset or your worst liability at trial. Try to interview them before you subpoena them. Evaluate their testimony and ask if it helps your case. If it does, get them under subpoena and use them; if not, don't.

You may want to TRY to interview hostile witnesses, including the cop or side-kick cop, to see what their testimony would be. If they don't want to talk with you, don't push at all. At trial just ask them the question, "Officer, did you refuse to answer my questions on [date]?" But be very careful subpoenaing hostile witnesses.

OK—you've got your:

1) Legal Folder

   a) statutes

   b) elements

   c) cases

2) Physical Evidence Folder

   a) diagrams

   b) photos

3) Testimony Folder

   a) your statement

   b) witness statements

      1) friendly

      2) neutral

      3) hostile

Now you want to start developing a game plan:

1) Do you have an affirmative defense? This would be if the prosecution proved everything they alleged and you could still win your case. There are two types, a legal defense and a factual defense.

   A) Legal Defense (relies heavily on Legal Folder) These are cases like:

      1) the wrong code section cited

      2) outside the jurisdiction of the court

      3) legal necessity (never works)

4)   double jeopardy

B)   Factual Defense (relies heavily on Physical Evidence or Testimony Folder)

1)   it wasn't you driving

2)   not on a highway

3)   not an unsafe speed

4)   the color of the light

5)   did stop

Factual defenses rely on the proof and credibility of you and your witnesses. The Court must disbelieve the cop and believe you. It happens. So just because it is the cop's word against your word, it may not be an impossible situation.

2)   Will your case rely on the prosecution's inability to prove the case against you?

A)   The prosecution might miss or fail to prove an element against you.

B)   You have to block testimony or evidence against you, preventing the prosecution from proving their case. (This is where and why OBJECTIONS are used.)

Until you actually get to trial, there is no real way to know if the prosecution is going to screw up. That's why it's never wrong to take a case to trial. Keep good notes and listen carefully to see if they omit an element or if your objections have kept out an element.

You may want to work up some general areas and types of questions to ask the witnesses and officer on cross-examination. Be flexible; don't write a script.

Gather all this stuff and think about it, then put it back in the folders and leave it there. Don't let this case consume too much of your energy or your time.

Chapter Seven

THE MORNING OF THE TRIAL

About the time that you feel good about your case as you drive to the courthouse, the symptoms start to set in. Elevated blood pressure, heightened anxiety, little beads of sweat . . . it's that chronic disease known to all ticket fighters:

"Whatif-itis"

"Whatif-itis" is the common feeling that you should have done something else, and that "they" know exactly what this is. It goes something like this.

What if (choose your favorites):

the cop shows up?

the cop doesn't show up?

the prosecution rests its case?

I can't think of any questions to ask the cop?

I can't remember what my case is about?

I don't have an argument?

(or the worst) they start laughing at me and I don't know why?

"Whatif-itis" is a relative of stage fright. Everyone will have some degree of it. Knowing it is normal may not make it go away, but at least you'll be better able to deal with it. Just keep the reasons why you wanted to fight this thing, along with the facts that told you to go ahead, out in front of you.

When you finally get enough nerve to get out of the car and walk up the courthouse steps, there is no one and nothing inside to help you ease that anxious feeling. Your name may be posted, directing you to a courtroom. You're on time and they make you wait. The courtroom is cold and impersonal. The police may be there but segregated from the defendants. Then you feel like the title on the ticket is true: It is in fact the whole "People of the State of (wherever) versus You." Now you really want to run.

Instead, come prepared. You know you're going to have to wait, so read a good book, do homework, organize your Rolodex—any of those things that you always say you never have the time to do. In addition to actually enjoying that little gift you're giving yourself, you'll also have the satisfaction of having them watch somebody who's actually using the time productively. It'll drive the cops nuts.

After the appropriate time-wasting period, the District Attorney (D.A.) may approach you in the hallway or waiting room. He'll ask you if you want to discuss your case. Finally, someone to talk to. Some person is taking an interest in you and your case. You want to relieve your stress and this D.A. is just the person.

You're just beaming with pride from the knowledge you have of the law, the great preparation you've made with charts, diagrams and witnesses you've got under subpoena. Now you can dazzle this person without the anxiety of a trial.

WRONG!!!

Didn't you ever watch "Perry Mason"? The D.A. is the bad guy here, the villain! He is not your friend who is idly chatting about your case. He has specific purposes.

1. Right off the bat, he is testing to see how serious you are. Maybe he can even talk you out. Don't buy it. No matter how friendly he is, court is an adversarial process, and the D.A. is on the other side.

2. Once he sees your resolve, he'll try to get you to reveal your facts right then so that:

   a. If you have a valid affirmative defense, the D.A. may try to negate it before you get to produce it in court. (If you think your case is so good that you could convince the prosecutor to dismiss it in the hallway, then it will be good enough to convince the judge at the trial.)

   b. If you have just an "okay" defense, it will tip him off to make sure he covers all his bases.

Either way, there is usually very little advantage in discussing your case with the prosecution.

Special Tip:

By all means, tell him that you have charts, diagrams, research, the works; but don't show him anything! Show him that you're serious without revealing your case. That way, he may sweeten the hallway deal enough to meet your minimum standards. Find out about his case.

That said, there are more settlements on all kinds of cases made in the hallways of the courthouse than any other place on earth. The key is to think your options through before you get to the hallway and set your limits on what would be an acceptable offer.

This person may offer you a chance to go to Traffic School—but you have already evaluated that option before now, and hallway pressure should not change your previous decision. But do what is best for YOU. If you have no affirmative defense and you see the officer sitting in court, MAYBE Traffic School is a good option at this time. But make it an objective decision, not one based on last-minute cold feet about going to trial.

The second alternative offered is usually a reduction of fine. Justice on sale. This is usually not as attractive an offer as it first seems because all the negative consequences will still be forthcoming, i.e., conviction, DMV point, insurance increase. Your time has already been invested in your case and that is worth more than the reduction of the fine. But, again, do what is in your best interest. If he offers a reduction in the charges from a moving violation to a parking ticket, then you may want to accept the reduction because this is what you hope your final result will be.

If they start giving away the courthouse, they may know that they won't be able to prove their case and that they will lose at trial. They won't tell you that. This is where the poker player has the advantage—look deep into their eyes and see if they are bluffing. Call their bluff and see if they can prove their case, or run with the best offer.

DO WHAT IS BEST FOR YOU; DO NOT SUC-
CUMB TO THE PRESSURE OF THE HALLWAY.

O.K., you did good. You didn't give away your case, but you're still nervous about the trial.

Then the judge walks in and everyone stands. End of another illusion, right then. Judges (with very few exceptions) are not the friendly, warm, compassionate, all-wise people that you had envisioned. The courtroom is a cold and threatening place, and you are uncomfortable. You don't fit in.

"Whatif-itis" again! This is your trial and you are getting cold feet. What are you doing here? You hate talking in front of people. You're not an attorney and don't really want to be here. Besides all that, you know you're guilty, if not of this one, then of something much worse than this one. You don't have time to waste sitting in court. The judge has heard it before, as well as the prosecution, the bailiff and the cop. You've talked with the prosecution, and they gave you a chance to go to Traffic School. What a fool you would be not to accept such a generous offer. Or they've indicated that they would cut the fine in half. Save money. You've sort of won. Isn't this, after all, a financial game? (Your rational brain is yelling, "Plead, Plead.")

The judge calmly announces that 80% to 90% of cases tried are not legal issues, and there is no chance of winning. You're now in a full sweat, panicked, and you want to run.

So what do you do? Starting with your own mind, TAKE CONTROL! Calmly remind yourself that:

1) You know your case better than anyone else in the universe. You've spent more time preparing this case than anyone in the courtroom. That knowledge is a powerful tool because it will allow you to detect flaws in their case as well to as present yours.

2) With that knowledge you may also know that you're guilty. Well, there is also an advantage there: "You can't lose a loser." That statement takes a lot of pres-

sure off you; you don't have to win. If the "truth" comes out, you'll be found guilty, and that's the worst thing that can happen.

3) No one is going to jail (unless you really tick off the judge). In an infraction case, the court does not have the power to put someone in jail, and they can usually only fine you up to a certain maximum.

4) Sure, all the world seems to be against you (the judge, the prosecution and the cop), but look around in court at all those other people who are silently on your side. They have the same fears and anxieties as you. They would love to see you, or anyone, win a case, or just give a good show.

5) You have nothing to lose. All the bad stuff will happen anyway if you "plead guilty with an explanation." DMV will give you a point, and your insurance company will know about it. Keep this in perspective. You may have been going 70/55—you just don't want it on your record. At trial, the only two options are Guilty or Not Guilty, and they can only say "Guilty" once.

6) It can be fun just playing the game, and it's even more fun if you win. So remind yourself of just how much fun you're having in the middle of all these sour people.

Finally, you will get nervous and begin to doubt. I should have done this . . . I should have looked up more of the law . . . I need a picture of the intersection from the northwest corner. Put all that aside—you have what you have and that will be good enough. You only have to win one stage—the prosecution has to win every time. Your case isn't going to get any better, and you're not going to get any smarter—SO JUST DO IT!

Keep the prosecution guessing where you're going. Don't engage in any further dialogue at this point, and don't try to be friends with him. Courteous, yes; friendly, no! As you nervously sit there, take a deep breath and smile when they call your case and you say, "Ready for trial, Your Honor!"

The trial—this is why we're here. You want to break down the trial into manageable chunks.

The case is called; the cop and prosecution answer, "Ready". It is now.

What are you going to say and do?

Chapter Eight

THE TRIAL AND "RALFY"

Meet "RALFY." He's going to help you get and keep your head screwed on straight about the main event of this whole process . . . the TRIAL.

R-A-L-F-Y

RALFY reminds us that the best way to get to "Not Guilty" is to start at the end:

Result = Not Guilty.

Argument = Reasonable doubt/insufficient evidence/ cop lied.

Law = What element didn't the prosecution prove?

Fact = What did the evidence show?

You = You will win because you know your case better than they do.

You are in the unique position of being both an attorney (representing yourself) and a witness. You must keep these two functions separate in your case and in your mind. When you act as an attorney, you can only do attorney things, and as a witness, you can only do witness things. The same goes for the other side. The D.A. can't testify to facts and the cop can't act as an attorney. Separate each part in its own separate "chair." As your own attorney, don't let the knowledge get in the way of your defense.

Now, get this. The trial isn't what happened out on the street. "The truth" is what is proven in court at the trial. Here are the only scenarios to be played out in a trial:

1. The prosecution doesn't prove their entire case; then you can win even if you were actually guilty.

2. You're guilty, and they prove it.

3. You're innocent, but the cop testifies to prove their case against you, and you are found guilty anyway.

4. You're innocent and you prove it.

Any combination of facts can result in any given verdict. So just because you are guilty doesn't mean you'll be found guilty, any more than being innocent means that you will be found not guilty. That's where RALFY comes in. Work backwards from the result you want to achieve, then go find the things that fit that result. (You'd be surprised how well this works in your everyday life as well!)

Unfortunately, trials are structured in the opposite order, so let's get back to your morning in court. Sometimes a list is posted that lets you know in what order your case will be called. No matter what it says, don't get excited. You could be number two, and the first case could take two hours. Or you could be number 26, and the first 25 could take 20 minutes. Other factors, like a continued case or a whiny lawyer like me, could change the order entirely. Whatever happens, don't let this stuff get under your skin. It's just all part of the "wear-you-down" game that they hope results in your being so fatigued that you'll plead anything just to get it over with. But with your good book, portable Monopoly game, or back checkbooks in hand, you will have already won a little victory. You will have taken the time they intended you to waste and made it very useful for yourself.

Finally, your turn is up. Each stage of a trial is broken down into distinct segments where you will be allowed to do certain things and not allowed to do others. This is not a normal thought process. Basically, the steps of a typical trial include:

1) Bailiff/court clerk calls the case.

2) You and prosecution answer, "Ready, your honor."

3) Witnesses are sworn in.

4) Opening arguments:

    a.   Prosecution

    b.   Defense

5) Prosecution's case:

    a.   Witness's, i.e, officer's, testimony

    b.   Witness's cross examination

    c.   Paper evidence:

        1.   Documents (e.g., the ticket)

    2. Charts/diagrams

    3. Other physical evidence

6) Motion(s) for dismissal (by you).

7) Defendant's case:

    a. Witnesses, i.e., you (your story)

    b. Prosecution's cross examination

    c. Paper evidence:

        1. Documents

        2. Charts/diagrams

        3. Other physical evidence

8) Defense rests.

9) Any rebuttal witnesses (by the prosecution).

10) Rebuttal by defense.

11) Closing arguments:

    a. Prosecution

    b. Defense

    c. Prosecution

12) Verdict.

13) If guilty, sentencing.

Each segment has its own place and time to be incorporated in the trial. Depending on the particular court and trial, not every step may be followed exactly. That's why seeing the court at work prior to the trial is such a good idea.

Step 1—Court Clerk Calls the Case

With RALFY at your side, you are already on the offensive (remember, you only have to win once). Immediately take note of all the players. The judge and the prosecutor are there (you can't start without them), but now is the time to take careful note of the witness(es).

> *Chance to Win No. 1:   Chances are about one in three that the cop won't show up. Without their "star" witness, you've won! Case dismissed.*

Step 2—"Ready, your honor."

That simple word "READY" has a lot of options attached to it.

If the prosecution requests a continuance to bring in the officer, you "object" to such a continuance (more on "objecting" a bit later). The court has the authority to grant a continuance over your objection. You may want to point out to the Court that the prosecution had known, or should have known, of the conditions prior to today and gave you NO NOTICE of the motion for the continuance.

If the judge seems like a decent enough person, you might try this. Tell the judge that you have taken off work and are ready today, and it would be inconvenient for you to come back. In effect, you have already paid a "fine" in terms of the time and energy spent. Finally, you had your act together and the prosecution didn't. The court should dismiss your case.

Unless there are extraordinary circumstances, the court MUST get you to trial within 45 days of your arraignment. Count 45 days from your first appearance where you pled Not Guilty. If you haven't "waived time," the court must get you to trial on or before the 45th day (or the working day after the 45th if it is a Saturday, Sunday or legal holiday) or they must dismiss the case.

If the court seems inclined to continue the matter over your objection, you may want to "waive time" for your own convenience. Otherwise you may have to accept the new date that the court dictates.

It's a two-way street. You may want a continuance for an unavailable witness or some other valid reason. Don't rely on a granted continuance just because you asked; the court can deny the request and you have to go to trial. That's O.K. Be ready to go to trial anyway.

Okay, say the cop is there and you're ready to go. The minute the clerk says "People vs. (your name)," the judge will ask if you are ready.

In a firm, confident voice, you say, "Ready, Your Honor." That lets the court know you are actually going to trial, and your resolve might send a message to the prosecutor that you've got your act together. Knowing that he's got sixteen more cases to handle, you might intimidate him just enough to have him go for an early acquittal, if only to get you out from under his nose.

Your tone is even worth practicing. Remember, answer firm and confident, not wimpy and tentative, and not angry or sarcastic. Use a positive and firm tone throughout the trial, and you might even surprise yourself.

Reminders:

Be ready and go for it—you have nothing to lose.

Take notes.

Make objections.

Ask questions.

Make the prosecution prove the case.

Be truthful—don't hang yourself. If there is a conflict, don't testify.

Your testimony is just as valid as the cop's.

Step 3—Witnesses Are Sworn In

Again, this is straightforward stuff, and nothing to get intimidated about. You are going to tell the truth, and you know the facts best, so you are the most confident person there. The cop is only reading from his notes, plus he's probably a little annoyed that he has to be there for such a minor matter anyway. Good for you. His apathy is your ally.

Step 4—Opening Statement

Sometimes this step will be omitted in traffic court, and you will have noticed it from watching other trials. But this part is no big deal anyway. It just a statement of what each side intends to do.

But if the court does have opening arguments, it helps at this point to understand the roles of the players. Although they are supposed to run the trial, the majority of judges that I have seen really assume you are guilty, although no one will ever say it out loud. Since the LAW says you are presumed innocent, everyone knows that if you're charged with 70/55, you're not guilty—RIGHT?

WRONG! You have an uphill battle to try to convince the Court otherwise. It can be done, and you can usually do it by preventing the prosecution from presenting its case.

So, rather than having the Court conduct business as usual, you want them to conform to their own rules. The Court may want to take an informal attitude, as in "this is the way we do it down here." You, on the other hand, want to keep it formal and make them jump through each legal hoop, because if they miss one—you win!

The Police Officer is ONLY a witness. He CANNOT participate in the trial except for testifying to the FACTS, such as what he saw or heard.

Many courts have just you and the judge and the cop (no prosecuting District Attorney.)

Fine. The cop can testify as to what the facts are, but:

CANNOT argue the case;

CANNOT comment on why the Judge should believe him;

CANNOT make a motion before the Court. The cop is not an attorney, nor does he represent the People. DO NOT let the cop act as prosecution.

ON THE OTHER HAND, you are an attorney for yourself (IN PRO PER), and that allows you to be both a witness (like the cop) and an attorney (like the prosecution). You can testify and argue your case. The cop can only testify and the prosecutor can only be an attorney. You must use both aspects to your advantage, maximizing your role while minimizing the cop's or prosecutor's roles.

The Court may try to allow the cop to act like the prosecutor. Try to prevent that from happening, and "object" when it does.

Prosecution's Opening Statement

In your "attorney" mode, this is NOTE-TAKING TIME. You're looking for obvious holes in the prosecutor's statement and to see if he misstates the evidence. He is bound to the evidence only, and his opinion has no place in the statement; he can only state fact and law and argue the case from what evidence (fact) applies to the law.

Try not to interrupt the prosecution during the statement, but note everything down. You'll have your chance shortly.

Your Opening Statement

An opening statement just describes what you intend to prove in your case. You will normally waive this because you don't want to give away your defense—or, more accurately, you may not know what your defense is until after you hear the prosecution's case.

You may not win the case, but you want to give the prosecution every opportunity to lose it.

Believe it or not, you can actually make a statement by not making a statement. When called upon for your opening statement, even if the prosecution gave one, reply firmly and confidently, "No, thank you, your honor."

I've seen lots of trials in which defendants try to use their opening statements to actually try the case, hoping the judge will see that they "obviously" didn't do it. On the other hand, the assertiveness of this simple response will convey that you are confident and not intimidated by this process. Already, you're telling everyone that you are different from over 90% of other defendants (unless they read this book, too).

If you do choose to file an opening statement, be concise. Just state your intentions and do not attempt to try the case.

Step 5—Prosecution's Case

The people must prove their case against you before you have to respond to anything. Your main objective is LEGALLY to prevent that from happening.

1. You want to hold the prosecution to its burden of proof.

2. You want to make sure only admissible evidence gets in.

3. You want to disrupt the set plan of action. The cop and the court are comfortable with their normal procedure. They will (with amazing speed if you let them) convict you in the normal course of business. You have to slow them up.

If there is no D.A. present, the cop will testify as if telling the judge a story.

You should say, "OBJECT, NARRATIVE." You have a right to find out if a question would call for an objectionable answer. If the cop is allowed to tell a story, then you don't know if his testimony would be excluded.

The prosecution's case will primarily, if not exclusively, be the police officer's testimony. If the prosecutor is there, it will take the form of a QUESTION-AND-ANSWER exchange between the prosecutor and the cop. If it is only the cop without a prosecutor, the testimony will be a narrative; the cop will tell the story.

At this point in the trial your function is as an attorney, and your plan of action is to:

1) **Take notes.** Draw a line down the center of a sheet of paper. On the left, take down in short notes the officer's testimony. Use the right for your objections, cross-examination or motions.

2) **Make objections** (see below).

3) **Look for elements not established**.

Okay, okay. You've heard this "objection" thing a few times now. Let's take a short course in . . .

"Your Honor, I Object!"

An objection simply calls into question some procedural aspect of the trial. The problem is that things that can or can't be done need to be objected to in order for the judge to act on them.

For example, during direct examination, you should object at least once or twice, just to throw the cop off his story.

Here's an example:

The cop testifies that he is a Highway Patrolman, 12-year veteran, who was on duty and in uniform patrolling on I–15. He first observed a car traveling at a high rate of speed . . . "Objection, your honor," you calmly state. "The witness is looking at notes." The judge sustains (agrees with you), and the cop has to put the notes away.

Just as you hear on "L.A. Law" all the time, the range of usual objections is fairly limited:

1. Hearsay

2. Foundation

3. Relevance

4. Immaterial

5. Speculation

6. Calls for a conclusion

7. Expert opinion; witness not qualified

Do not be too concerned about the technical definitions, and whether it's proper or not. Take it from the experts—object and guess at a reason. Let the judge figure out if it's proper or not. That's his/her job. When in doubt, stand up and say "Objection, Your Honor!"

If the judge "OVERRULES" your objection, you lose and the answer can come in. If the judge "SUSTAINS" your objection, you win and the answer stays out. Since the judge can't keep out improper evidence unless you make the objections, object early and often.

The real and primary purpose of objections is to limit the testimony of the witness to only admissible evidence. If you can prevent a crucial element from being introduced into evidence, then you can win the case.

A closer look at these objections:

Hearsay

Hearsay is an out-of-court statement offered to prove the truth of the matter. Law students get about a half of a semester devoted to this objection. For you, it's simple: Hearsay is anything *said or written* outside the courtroom.

Here's a common example. It's an accident case.

A witness on the scene told the cop, who wrote it down in the report, what happened. Now the cop is going to read from his report what happened at the accident.

You say "Objection, 'Hearsay.'" Clearly this is hearsay. The witness who said those words must testify. The cop can't testify to what a document says. If you even see the cop pick up a document, this should be hearsay.

Foundation

There's nothing to back up what the cop is saying (e.g., calibration for speedometer).

Irrelevant

This is all the stuff that might have happened but has nothing to do with the *application of the law as it directly relates to this case.*

Some examples of irrelevant testimony:

Your attitude at the stop.

Other violations that the cop didn't write down.

The fact that he was writing lots of speeding tickets that day (the "full moon" theory of law enforcement).

Immaterial

Similar to "Irrelevant"; may have some connection to the case at hand, but too remote to be useful, e.g., your past driving record.

Speculation

Asking the cop to guess about something he wouldn't otherwise be able to know. Examples:

"He probably had a fight with his wife."

"He could clearly see the red light."

"He was really mad. He's lucky I didn't arrest him for disorderly conduct." (Speculation *and* Irrelevant)

Conclusion

Asking the witness (or the witness attempting on his or her own) to conclude something that he or she has no basis to conclude; e.g., the prosecution asks, "The car was swerving and the driver had slurred speech. Did he seem drunk to you, Officer?"

Not Qualified; Needs an Expert Witness

Asking the witness (or the witness attempting on his or her own) to conclude something that he or she doesn't have the expertise to determine. Examples:

"He was acting 'crazy.'" (Witness is not a psychologist)

"His front end was out of alignment." (Witness is not a professional mechanic)

During the prosecution's case, you can't testify or ask questions, but note it all down and you will get an opportunity to do so during the trial. BE PATIENT—the only thing you're allowed to do is make LEGAL objections. So OBJECT!

Here are two of my all time favorite objections:

RALFY'S All-Star Objection No. 1

This is an objection that almost always works. It's also a darn good legal strategy.

The cop will have the citation in front of him, and will look down at it from time to time. Object to this. The cop has to testify from "independent recollection" and reading off his citation is not the correct way to testify.

You OBJECT and request that he put the notes away. The court usually instructs the officer to put away his notes, but will allow him to refer to the notes during his testimony to "refresh his recollection."

This gives you a great advantage. Now you have a copy of the evidence the cop should testify to. If he deviates from the written citation, you can use whatever is more favorable to your case as evidence. If what he says on the witness stand is more favorable, use that. If what is on the ticket is more favorable, you can, on cross-examination, use it to impeach his testimony.

If the officer is allowed to use the citation to testify, you have a right to look at whatever the officer has used to "refresh his memory."

Request of the court that you be allowed to look at what the cop has written down. You know that it is the citation, but you might be surprised as to what he has written on the back of it. Take a look at the citation. Either the marshall or bailiff will take it from the cop and hand it to you.

Watch the cop's face. You may not win the case, but the look you get may be worth the whole trial.

This may be the time to go for the jugular. You can win the case if the officer does not have "independent recollection" of the events of the day he issued the citation.

The Sixth Amendment of the U.S. Constitution gives you the right TO BE CONFRONTED WITH THE WITNESSES AGAINST YOU.

IT IS THE COP'S TESTIMONY, NOT THE CITATION, THAT MUST CONVICT YOU. If the cop has no "independent recollection" of the events, then he is "INCOMPETENT TO TESTIFY AS A WITNESS" because he has "NO PERSONAL KNOWLEDGE" of the events. If the court allowed the citation into the record, then all defendants would be guilty as soon as the citation was written.

Here's how you get the cop to admit he has no "independent recollection":

Q. "Officer, as you sit on the stand today, can you recall the events of the citation?"

Q. "After referring to your notes, have you now refreshed your recollection and do you have a present recollection of the events of the day?"

Q. "Without the notes, would you be able to testify?"

Q. "After reviewing your notes, can you testify from your present memory?"

Q. "Are you relying exclusively on your notes to testify today?"

If he answers "Yes" to the final question, request a dismissal from the court at this time. If it is granted, you win. If the court does not grant the dismissal, limit the officer's testimony only to what is written on the ticket—NOTHING MORE!

If the citation reads "SI5," the cop should be allowed to testify only to "SI5," not "South on Interstate 5."

If the cop does state that he now has "independent recollection," don't offer the citation back to him. Ask him to proceed with his testimony. See how long it takes for him to ask for his copy of the ticket back.

It's a fun objection—use it.

RALFY'S All-Star Objection No. 2

Now, as the officer testifies and is coming close to the key element of the case, you want to object just before he tries to nail you.

It doesn't matter what the objection is; just object.

This will stop the proceedings and require the judge to rule. So what if he rules against you. The officer may have thought he testified to the critical information and forget to testify. You win.

Paper Evidence

The prosecution may try to get in documents against you; object to them on Foundational Grounds and/or Hearsay. They must be proper or the documents are inadmissible. If the prosecution has identified either documents or pictures that they want to introduce into evidence, they must:

1) Mark the document for ID.

2) Have a witness identify what it is.

3) Admit the document into evidence.

If you can keep out the evidence, then it cannot be used against you.

After the prosecution has presented their evidence, they will announce, "The people rest." That is your cue to ask for a dismissal of the charges because:

1) The prosecution has not identified you as the driver of the vehicle.

2) The court is without jurisdiction because it was not established that the offense was within the jurisdiction of the court.

3) The prosecution has left out an element of the offense charged:

   a) No speed ever cited.

   b) Color of the light not established.

   c) Any fact that they omitted or misstated that is important to their case.

4) The act does not establish a violation charged (wrong code section).

If the prosecution tries to RE-OPEN to establish the missing element, OBJECT to the re-opening.

Try to be as specific as possible, but if you can't think of anything they left out, make the motion anyway. The judge may have seen something you missed and grant the motion. Then it's over.

Remember—you only have to win once.

The prosecution will finish their testimony. Ask yourself three important questions:

Does the prosecution have enough evidence to convict me?

Has the prosecution left out an element of the offense?

Did the prosecution identify me in court?

You may have a winner at this point, and may not want to risk asking any questions of the cop. If you want to rely on the state of the evidence, right now ask no questions and let THE PEOPLE REST. Then ask the court to dismiss the case.

If the motion is granted, you win. If the motion is not granted, you go on with your case. Remember, you only have to win once; the prosecution has to win every time.

Cross-Examination of Cop

If you don't think you can win the case at the close of the direct examination, it is important to have an effective cross-examination against the police officer. You must cross-examine in the form of questions. The officer's testimony will usually be sufficient evidence to convict you. Therefore, you must bring out from the officer: 1) reasonable doubt; 2) a question as to the credibility of his testimony.

There are two rules for every question you will ask (the same two rules that the prosecution just used on you): 1) You already know the answer to the question, and 2) the answer to that question will help your case.

Too often, I've seen otherwise well-prepared people remember the first rule but forget the second. Here are some examples:

"How fast was I going?"

"What color was the light?"

Asking questions of the ultimate fact will always elicit a guilty response. The cop would not have shown up if he thought the ticket was bogus. What you want to show on cross-examination is that the officer's credibility is suspect, hence, reasonable doubt exists.

When the officer testifies, he is ONLY a witness, and the court should evaluate his testimony exactly like anyone else's. In California, the law says, "In determining the believability of a witness, you (the court) may consider anything that has a tendency in reason to prove or disprove the truthfulness of the testimony of the witness, including but not limited to any of the following:

(1) "The extent of the opportunity or the ability of the witness to see or hear or otherwise become aware of any matter about which the witness has testified;" (CALJIC 2:20)

Here's the right way to question. Phrase questions to test the officer's observation:

How long did the officer have to observe the action (in seconds, minutes, miles)?

Was he doing something else (your donut question)?

What was his exact location in relation to the site of the alleged offense?

(2) "The ability of the witness to remember or to communicate any matter about which the witness has testified;" (CALJIC 2:20)

Phrase the questions to test his memory. The smaller the detail the better. Ask specific questions about your car, such as, Does it have a sun roof? What color is the car? Followed by, What shade of _____? Did the car have any unusual features or characteristics (eg., mag wheels, a big dent, a hood scoop, etc.)?

The officer will have the basic description of the car from the ticket—make, model, color and license plate number. He may know that the car is blue because it's on the citation, but can't remember if it is two-tone or paneled. The more you can get him to say, "I don't know," the weaker the testimony.

Just remember, the strength of your case lies in framing the right questions. Any answer helps.

Let's take the car color question. Your car is light blue. You ask the cop, "What color was the car?"

If the cop says	Then you've got
"The car was blue."	No problem. The "What shade of blue" question will get you where you want to go.
"I don't know."	Double score for you. First, his testimony is weakened because he can't remember. Second, he's dumb because he can't even remember what he wrote on the ticket.
"It was red."	He lies, you may win.

The point is, the right question doesn't hurt you, will probably help you, and might even give the prosecution a chance to win your case for you.

Okay, back to your cross examination. Ask about the other cars in the area. Again, phrase the question (or series of questions) to get the "I don't know" response.

For example, ask, "Officer, did you see the van in the #2 lane?"

Don't ask, "Were there any other cars around?"

He'll answer the first question, "I don't know," which hurts his credibility. But to the second question he could simply answer, "No," which just pits your word against his.

Also, ask questions that start with, "Isn't it a fact that . . ." You are implying that the fact exists and you are testing him on it. Even if you don't win, this could be the most satisfying part for you: giving the cop back everything he gave you on the street.

Next, ask questions concerning the physical layout of the street (because you have charts, diagrams or pictures of the area and they don't).

"How far?"

"How wide?"

"Any trees?"

"How many?"

"Anything that would impede your vision?"

Anything that will test his observations. This is a wonderful set of questions, because if he slips up, you will have proof of what the layout actually is. If he answers correctly, you haven't lost anything and it shows the court that you represented the area correctly.

3) "The character and quality of that testimony;" (CAL-JIC 2:20)

How has the testimony stood up against the actual facts?

4) "The demeanor and manner of the witness while testifying;" (CALJIC 220)

This is your tool for the cop with the attitude problem. But be careful here. Some of the most obnoxious cops out on the street will put on their two-faced, sweet, "I'm just doing my job" face in court.

Out on the street the cop is in charge. When you get him in court on cross-examination, YOU are in charge. He MUST answer your questions. This is where you can try to get to him, and show the court that this person may be going beyond his authority; or just for fun, get him upset.

For example, if the cop starts to go beyond the question, you can cut him off by saying the answer is "non-responsive."

Or ask the officer, "Didn't you say this to me on the evening of July 11, 1993?" Or, "Isn't it a fact that you called me a 'snot-nosed, pimple-faced jerk' when you stopped me?"

> 5) "The existence or nonexistence of a bias, interest, or their motive;" (CALJIC 2:20)

The officer will try to put across to the court that, "Hey, I'm just doing my job, why should I lie about the facts?"

Yeah, right! Cops do have biases, and some can even be called into question.

If the officer is a Highway Patrol or Traffic Officer, his job is to enforce the vehicle code. The way he knows whether or not he is doing his job is by the number of tickets he writes. They will *never* admit there is a quota system in their department, but they will admit that they turn in so many tickets a month, or that they are evaluated in part on the number of tickets written.

Ask the cop if he knows whether the Police Department gets any portion of the fine collected from traffic citations issued by them.

Ask if they are getting paid for their testimony, or if they get "comp time" for the testimony in court.

Of course, they are getting paid for coming to court, and it could show bias, interest or motive.

If the judge is to use the above criteria to evaluate the testimony of the witnesses, you must be aggressive in your cross-examination of the officer. Make notes on the officer's testimony, especially if you got him riled, to use in final argument.

If you get too many responses of "I cannot recall at this time," and the officer is starting to sound like he really doesn't get it, you can go for a winner right now.

Another use of cross-examination is to prove your case. If you can get enough "facts" from the officer, you may not need to testify (e.g., the "red" car in his testimony that is blue on the ticket).

As the "F" in RALFY asks:

What do you want to prove?

Can you get this from the officer's testimony?

Can you create a reasonable doubt in the judge's mind?

After your cross-examination, the prosecution will have an opportunity to ask questions of the officer on re-direct.

This will be to try to rehabilitate the officer's credibility after your questioning.

Listen to the questions carefully, because they will give you insight into what the prosecution deems important and where they think their problems are in the case.

The prosecution can ask only questions that you have inquired about. This may become important if the prosecution has left out an element of the offense the first time around or has not identified you.

You have to say, "OBJECT, Your Honor, the question is beyond the scope of cross-examination." The response to this objection may give you an indication that the court will dismiss the charges at the end of the prosecutor's case—because an element or identity has not been established.

You will also be able to ask questions on what the prosecution has covered in re-direct examination.

As before, you should object on re-direct and ask questions on re-cross-examination.

At this point, the prosecution may try to introduce documents against you; object to them on Foundational Grounds and/or grounds of Hearsay. They must be proper or the documents are inadmissible.

Step 6—Motions by the Defendant

This is a very powerful tool that you must wait to use. It's also a great way for you to remind yourself of the power that you own. At the close of the People's case, be sure that they say the words "THE PEOPLE REST." That closes the door on them submitting additional evidence.

Chance to Win No. 2: Once the People rest, you can request the Court to dismiss the case because of insufficient evidence. It is your TIME OUT. Once you request a dismissal, the Court must rule on the state of the evidence at the close of the People's case. If they have left out an element of the case, you win. If they did not identify you, you win. If there are not

sufficient grounds to con-
vict you, you win. This is a
'no lose' situation for you.

Make the motion, and see what happens.

Step 7—Defendant's Case

Okay, the judge does not dismiss the case. This is your chance to show all the knowledge and skill you've acquired.

The first and most important question is whether or not to testify. Most of my clients are so anxious to tell their story that they just assume they will testify. However, you MUST weigh the pros and cons of testifying before you proceed. Here are three questions you must answer:

1. Are you going to help or hurt your case by testifying?

2. Do you have enough to argue without testifying?

3. Do you want to submit yourself to cross-examination?

Here's how testifying can work against you. Let's say the charge is going 70 mph in a 55 mph zone. If you're going to testify that you weren't doing 70 mph, but you couldn't have been going over 60—you have just CON-VICTED yourself.

Don't be intimidated by the Court. YOU HAVE A RIGHT NOT TO TESTIFY AGAINST YOURSELF.

Of course, many of my clients think they have the option of stating that they were only doing 55 mph. WRONG! If you have an option of convicting yourself or lying under oath—DO NEITHER!

A Short Course in Ethics

In addition to being illegal, lying on the stand is just plain dumb. It could turn a simple traffic ticket into PERJURY, a misdemeanor offense. Even though it's just a traffic case, you were sworn in at the start of the trial, and your testimony is given under oath. Just ask yourself, Is this traffic ticket worth risking perjury for?

Now for the dumb part. Remember, the prosecutor is a professional trained in exposing lies. In cross examination, he can take that "little" lie and end up having you praying that a conviction on the traffic ticket is all you'll be facing. Once you lie, keeping the "facts" straight gets more and more complicated.

Politely ask the judge if you can take a moment to review the case so far (again, you are demonstrating your control of the situation). Has the prosecution proven their case? If they haven't, or if their case is weak, you may not want to testify because you could inadvertently supply them with the needed element to their case. You don't want to do that.

Do you want to subject yourself to cross-examination by the prosecutor (not the cop)? Your story may sound really good when you tell it, but when the prosecutor gets through with you on cross-examination, it may not sound too good.

What are your options?

1) Don't testify.

2) Have someone else testify.

3) Call the cop as your witness.

4) Testify.

You can get your evidence, such as diagrams or pictures, entered through the testimony of the cop or your witness.

If you testify, you have the option of limiting your testimony to only a specific area, e.g., the physical diagram—but let the Court and prosecution know you're only going to testify in that area. Then they can only cross-examine you on those questions.

"Your Honor, I will testify on the limited area of the physical diagram only."

Here's the other side of the "ethics" issue. If you do tell your side of the story, tell the truth. You have taken an oath to tell the truth; your integrity and peace of mind are more important than WINNING the case at all costs. The truth is also much easier to remember. Unlike the other side, you get to tell your side of the story from beginning to end, because now you are the WITNESS and the ATTORNEY at the same time.

You are now selling your credibility to the Court. If the Court believes you, you will win. Try to be as consistent with the cop as possible. However, there must be some points of difference between you and the cop, or most likely you'd convict yourself. Try to visualize a video tape of the incident and describe what you see and hear.

WITNESSES, in general, can only relate facts and give opinions (if qualified to do so). Facts are those things that come through the senses: eyes, ears, nose, etc. The witness must have personally observed the events and must have present recollections of the events.

Therefore, as a witness, you want to give facts. You'll argue those facts in your final arguments.

As for your diagrams, pictures, charts, documents, and so on, there is usually a set procedure for handling them:

1) Clerk marks them "A," "B," "C" for identification.

2) Let them be shown to the opposing side.

3) Identify the diagram as the intersection of X & Y.

4) Show the relevance to the case, e.g., "This is where the sign is posted."

5) Have the document "introduced into evidence." Make the diagram for your purpose; if there are trees, show trees. Also, don't show the diagram to the opposite side until you are putting on your case because:

   a) Their diagram may be better for your purpose than your diagram. Use theirs.

   b) Their diagram may be so blatantly wrong that it hurts their credibility.

Step 8—Defense Rests

At the end of your case you will have to declare that the "defense rests." Before you do, ask the Court to admit your evidence that was marked during trial. Say, "Offer to move into evidence all previously identified exhibits." This ensures that what you submitted will be considered. Then the "Defense Rests."

Steps 9 & 10—Rebuttal

Rebuttal is for both the prosecution and defense, and is exactly like the prosecution's and defendant's cases prior. However, NO NEW ISSUES can be presented. Everyone is limited to explaining or clarifying that which has already gone before. Don't let the cop get away with "Oh, I forgot to tell you that . . ." It's too late for that.

Step 11—Final Arguments

This is where you and "RALFY" team up. Become focused only on the result, then show how:

1) The state did not meet its BURDEN OF PROOF.

2) Reasonable doubt exists (witness credibility).

Therefore, there has been no violation of law. Notice how I never said whether you did or didn't do it.

Now this is where you have to be a little flexible. You don't want to write your argument before you hear the evidence.

Both you and the prosecutor can argue only those facts that were admitted into evidence at trial. That means you can't argue about what you could have brought or the evidence that was not admitted, nor about evidence stricken by the judge.

Also, in your closing argument, don't focus on *what* this or that witness said. Focus instead on *why* that testimony either proved your case or more importantly, failed to prove the prosecution's. This is important because the prosecution will have the last chance to argue.

That also means the state is limited to what is admitted into evidence. So if you have successfully prevented the prosecution from entering a statement or other evidence, they can't argue that in their closing argument, either. Rather than re-stating what a witness said, point out how what that witness said either supports your contention or causes doubt about the prosecution's contentions.

The prosecution will have the last chance to argue.

Defense Closing Argument

Acting in your "Attorney" mode, this is your opportunity to tell the judge why he or she should find you Not

Guilty. Tell him what the evidence shows. You will pick the argument from the evidence you've just heard, with a general theory that the cop may even have lied himself (you'd be amazed how often this happens). You may find that the prosecution left out an element of their case, and you can win it on "Burden of Proof," or "No Violation of Law." That's why it is important to listen during the trial to collect your bits and pieces for the argument.

Be careful not to talk too many "defenses." "Defenses" are critical points that you are going to try to build your case on. Usually, a more specific defense is better than a shotgun defense approach. Here are some typical defense points:

1) "It wasn't me."

2) "I wasn't going that fast."

3) "The cop is lying."

4) "His radar is inaccurate."

5) "The radar was accurate, the cop is telling the truth, I was going that fast and it was me, but my speed was still safe and reasonable under the circumstances."

Each one of these points may be a legitimate defense, but if you lump them all together, you're asking the court to believe that they've got one really screwed-up cop out there. Whether it's true or not, the court is not likely to agree.

Pick your strongest one or two defense points and use them. Here's the hard part. You can't decide which ones to use until you hear all the evidence and the prosecution's case. Be creative and flexible, and *do* cover all the points of your case.

There is a great tendency in the final argument to talk too much. Professional attorneys often make the same mistake, and it's roughly based on one of these theories:

1) If I keep talking, the judge will buy one of my arguments; or

2) As long as I keep talking, I'm not convicted; therefore I haven't lost, so I'll keep talking.

As much as it hurts, be direct and to the point.

Prosecution's Closing Argument

Sit back, take a deep breath, and enjoy your moment.

Don't be too worried about what the prosecutor says at this stage. They are limited to what's in the trial and what you have said. In fact, the more they talk, the more trouble their case is in.

You have just finished doing something the courts really wished you wouldn't do. In that sense, you have done a great job of beating the system, no matter what the outcome.

Congratulations!

Step 12—Verdict

Usually, the judge will just take a moment or two on the stand, then render a verdict right there. Good! Who needs any more hassle? And, just like on TV, it will be short and to the point:

Not Guilty (congratulations!), or

Guilty, in which case, keep reading.

Step 13—Sentencing

Sentencing is the time when the judge tells you what the fine is. The case is over. NO MORE ARGUING.

During the final phase you're emotionally upset. You've just gone through a very traumatic trial in which you believed you were right, and the judge (essentially calling you a liar) has found you guilty. You have to let it go and go on with life. (Every case I lose I feel I should appeal, but almost always let it rest.) Saying nothing is sometimes the best thing you can do for your case.

As your own "attorney," you have to be aware that the person (the judge) before whom you have been presenting your case now has broad discretion as to what your sentence will be. Since the case involves an infraction, the worst he can usually do is fine you. The judge, in almost all cases, can't put you in jail unless he finds you in contempt of court (you really ticked him off, a new charge). Just be polite and civil, BUT assertive, and you'll do fine.

You have a limited right to present evidence as to "mitigation." In lay terms, "mitigating" factors are those things that might make a situation not quite as bad as it seems. For example, let's assume that you did not testify. You can now tell the judge that you weren't doing 70 mph, but only 63 mph. During the trial a statement by you that you were going 63 mph would have been a confession, but going 63 mph is less than 70 mph, and now it can work for you as a mitigating factor.

If you've chosen not to testify, sentencing is a good time to tell the judge your case. It makes you human. It also lets the judge know that you took the oath seriously, and although you're now admitting guilt (a good strategy, since he just found you guilty), there were other factors concerning your case: Tell the judge.

Most sentences are standard in traffic cases. The amount of the bail will be the amount of the fine. However, with mitigating circumstances or a well-presented case, the fine could be substantially reduced or suspended (no fine). And, although you lost the war, i.e., were found guilty, you might win at least part of the battle.

Mitigating factors are a two-way street, though. The fine can go up if the facts at trial support it, or if the judge feels you were less than honest on the stand. The judge has already determined that the cop was telling the truth, and you were a lying defendant; the only issue now is how the judge is going to punish you. You gave the judge a blank check with your name signed on the bottom. That is why it is important during trial that you keep a perspective on "WHO'S GOING TO SENTENCE ME IF I GET CONVICTED?" It may change your trial tactics and strategy. No matter how much of a jerk the judge might be during the trial, he is still the person with the power.

Chapter Nine

CUSTOMIZING YOUR DEFENSE

Regardless of the jurisdiction, almost all traffic-related violations that we're going to deal with fall into one of five categories, three "moving" and two "non-moving." While the non-moving violations may include a fine, they usually do not carry the "point" penalty on your license.

Moving Violations

Speed

Most of the cases in traffic court concern the speed of the vehicle, either as unsafe speed or as exceeding the maximum speed limit. Each one requires a different approach to the defense.

Judgment

The next group of cases has to do with the driver's judgment. These cases might involve passing through a red light, following too close, unsafe lane changes, and other instances where the judgment of the driver is in question.

Signs

These are "failure to obey" types of violations, such as no U-Turn; right lane must turn right; stop sign, etc.

Non-Moving Violations

Safety

These are "paper" violations, usually having to do with the safety of the car. They are often "fix-it" violations, such as a broken headlight, inoperative seatbelt, etc.

Parking

Finally, you have parking violations: red zone, overtime, etc. These are rarely worth fighting unless either you have so many that the cost alone warrants a defense, or the tow/impound charges and other court-imposed penalties are out of hand.

To help keep our perspective, we'll focus on the moving violations. If you really need to fight the non-moving violations, the principles of evidence, especially in the "Sign" example, will apply.

Now we'll look at how all this trial stuff in Chapter 8 applies to particular types of tickets. As we go through the cases, I'll refer to the various steps we just learned. Keep in mind, this is not a by-the-numbers process. I can only give you examples based on successful defenses of hundreds of cases. You have to apply the principles in Chapters 8 and 9 to your own case.

Speeding Tickets

Example 1—The Freeway Ticket

Whether it's called a freeway, expressway, interstate or highway, we're talking about those limited-access, multi-lane strips of asphalt that we all just can't seem to hold to the posted speed limit on. The ticket is usually phrased something like "exceeding the maximum posted 55 mph zone."

You have to understand that more likely than not, you are NOT going to testify, RIGHT? Everyone knows you're guilty, RIGHT? The judge will drive home that night doing 70 in the 55 zone, right along with the cop (off duty), the bailiff and the clerk. Everyone does 70 in the 55 zone. The only difference is that you have the ticket and they don't.

If you testify, your choices are less appealing than you probably think:

1) "I wasn't going THAT fast. I was only doing 65, not 70 mph." You've just convicted yourself, because the charge is exceeding the 55 mph maximum speed law; so if you admit to doing *anything* over 55 mph, you've just at best made yourself a little less guilty, but guilty nonetheless. You're better off paying the fine and saving yourself the trial preparation time.

2) "I was going 55 mph." That will inherently be distrusted, because no one does 55 mph on the freeway, and if you did, the cop would more likely write you up for impeding traffic than for speeding. You're in a straight his-word-against-mine situation.

3) "My speedometer was broken." As Wayne would say, "NOT." If you can't tell how fast you're going, you shouldn't be driving in the first place.

Impossible dilemma? RALFY says no.

Remember what we said about "presumption of innocence?" Rather than admitting to anything, make them prove you were doing over 55 mph. It's the American way. Better yet, try to prevent the prosecution from proving their case.

Here are some specific tactics:

Step 1: When the judge calls our case, we answer, "Ready, Your Honor" (they like being called "Your Honor"), and pray like hell the cop isn't there.

Step 4: Opening Statements. No, because we have no idea what our defense is going to be.

Step 5: Prosecution. The prosecution calls their first witness. The cop's testimony will go something like this:

"I have been a highway patrol officer for 12 years. I was on duty on February 6, 1993 (the day of your ticket), in uniform, and in a marked vehicle in the County of Wherever. While on routine patrol I observed a vehicle, a Honda, blue in color, traveling on I–10 in excess of 55 mph."

Assuming he has made no major errors so far, now is the time to really start taking notes on his testimony. Even though he will talk fast, often in an unbroken sentence, I've broken the key areas down.

The cop continues, "I entered the Freeway,

- began a pace by positioning my patrol vehicle 150 feet to the right rear
- of the subject vehicle and
- obtained a reading of 70 mph."

At some point he will attempt to validate that reading.

- "My speedometer was calibrated on 2 January 93 (they love military dates) and was one mile off.

- At 70 mph reading it was an actual speed of 71 mph.

- After pacing the vehicle for 2½ miles, I activated my Red Light.

- The vehicle yielded to the right shoulder,

- where I issued a citation for 22349 VC, exceeding the maximum speed limit."

END OF TESTIMONY

Change the facts to suit your case. But if you did nothing, that's how the testimony would likely go. Now let's replay the same sequence, using the tools of law to which you're entitled:

Cop: I have been a highway patrol officer for 12 years. I was on duty on February 6, 1993 (the day of your ticket), in uniform, and in a marked vehicle in the County of Wherever. While on routine patrol I observed a vehicle, a Honda, blue in color, . . .

You: Objection, Your Honor. He seems to be reading from some notes. Would you have him put away his notes? He can use them to refresh his recollection, if need be.

The judge and cop look at you like you're nuts.

Judge: Of course he can look at his citation.

You: Thank you, Your Honor. Then would you let the record reflect that he is reading from the citation.

Judge: Officer, do you need your notes to testify?

Cop: I can testify without my notes.

He puts the citation aside. He continues.

Cop: I observed a blue Honda traveling eastbound on I–10 in excess of 55 mph. I entered the Freeway and began a pace. I positioned my vehicle 150 feet to the right rear of the subject's vehicle and obtained a reading of . . .

You: OBJECTION—NO FOUNDATION as to calibration of the speedometer.

D.A.:   Officer, was your speedometer calibrated?

Cop: My speedometer was calibrated on 1–2–93 . . .

You: OBJECTION—NO PERSONAL KNOWLEDGE or BEST EVIDENCE. The best evidence is the document, not what the officer says it is.

Was the cop present when calibration was done? Is there a document of the results of the calibration?

The cop then pulls out a copy of the calibration test! "OH, NO!" you think. The calibration is marked and placed into evidence. Annoyed now with all this trivia, the cop continues his testimony.

Cop: I paced the vehicle for 2½ miles and activated my Red Light. The vehicle yielded to the right shoulder where I issued a citation for 22349/VC, exceeding the maximum speed limit.

End of Testimony

D.A.:   Any questions by Defendant?

You: NO!

D.A.:   The People rest.

You: Your Honor, I would like to make a *Motion for Dismissal.*

Judge: On what grounds?

You: *First,* there was no identification of who was driving the vehicle. The officer only referred to the vehicle, not who was driving.

       Second, there has been no evidence of a violation of law: no testimony as to what speed the vehicle was traveling.

Judge: I'm going to allow the officer to re-open . . .

You: Objection, Your Honor, on several grounds. First, the People have rested and the Court can only consider the evidence already entered at this stage. Second, the officer is not an attorney and cannot make a motion to re-open.

Don't have any illusions about what might happen now. You're completely in the right and you've out-smarted the prosecution. But nobody, including the judge, likes to be shown up, especially by some smart-ass who's not even an attorney! So instead of a grateful court, expect something like this:

Judge: The Court overrules your objections and allows the officer to re-open.

Cop: I paced the defendant who is sitting in the blue shirt at counsel table (he identifies you) and got a reading of 70 mph . . .

Judge: Any questions of the Officer?

Your cross-examination. With bravado and arrogance, the judge has just tried to set you off. He would like nothing better than to get you mad so he could try for a contempt case. But instead, you reassert yourself with poise and confidence. You're in control and it's driving everyone crazy, except for you and everyone who is watching (and silently cheering).

> You: YES, YOUR HONOR! Officer, where was your first observation?

> Cop: At Jefferson Road.

> You: Were you stationary or moving?

> Cop: I was stopped at the top of the road.

> You: Where did you pull me over?

> Cop: At Washington Road.

> You: Did you rely on your speedometer to issue me the citation?

> Cop: Yes, along with my visual observation.

> You: Would you have written the citation based solely on the speedometer reading?

> Cop: No.

> You: Would you have written the citation based solely on your visual observation?

> Cop: No.

> You: Officer, who calibrated your speedometer?

> Cop: AAA.

> You: No. The question is, which person did the actual calibration of the speedometer?

> Cop: I don't know.

> You: What were the qualifications of the person who did the calibration?

> Cop: I don't know.

You: Your Honor, motion to strike the calibration of the speedometer.

Let's assume that the judge is still being a jerk.

Judge: Overruled.

He has tried again, but failed to shake you with his arrogance and stupidity. You've got the upper hand and he knows it. You continue.

You: Officer, what is the distance between Jefferson Road and Washington Road?

Cop: Three miles.

You: After you activated your Red Light, how far did it take to pull over to the side of the road?

Cop: One-half mile.

You: What was the highest speed you reached from Jefferson Road to Washington Road?

Cop: 70 mph.

You: What was the greatest distance between your vehicle and my vehicle?

Cop: One-quarter mile.

You: That was when you entered the freeway from a stop?

Cop: Yes.

You: Was the vehicle you paced going at a constant speed?

Cop: Yes.

You: It didn't change lanes?

Cop: No.

You: When did you close to 150 feet to begin your pace?

Cop: After I entered the freeway.

Notice how you are asking questions that you already know the answers to. That's why they are called "lawyers' questions."

You: Did you change lanes during the pace?

Cop: No.

You: There was other traffic on the Sunday afternoon, right?

Cop: None in the area.

At this point the cop is definitely sensing the heat. He's basically trying to build his case in front of the judge as he goes. Don't get overconfident here, or you might let him do it. You continue, more focused than ever.

You: No traffic for the three miles between Jefferson and Washington?

Cop: I don't recall.

You: Wasn't all the other traffic traveling at approximately the same speed?

Cop: I don't know.

You: Did you pass *any* other vehicle?

He's suddenly not sure that you don't have a witness in your back pocket that could make him into a perjurer. All of a sudden, he's making career decisions.

Cop: No. Ah, yes. I don't know.

You: Was there anyone else in my car?

Cop: I don't know. One . . . male, I think.

You: How old? Was he ten years old or 40?

Cop: I don't know.

You: No further questions, Your Honor.

Judge: Officer, did you want to add anything?

Cop: No. (He's had enough.)

This time, the PEOPLE really do REST.
YOUR CASE: Right off, you throw a curve.

You: No affirmative defense, Your Honor.

This means that you are not going to testify. You don't want to testify. If you say you were going 55 mph on a Sunday afternoon, no one is going to believe you; or you can testify you were ONLY doing 65 mph; or going with the flow of traffic; or your speedometer wasn't working; or you didn't know it was a 55 mph zone. None of these are LEGAL excuses and you will just have convicted yourself.

Better to remain silent and let the cop be a fool than to testify and risk taking his place.

ARGUMENT: You do have plenty to argue, though, so you go straight to *Step 11: Closing Argument.*

"1)   The officer testified that he would not have written the ticket without the speedometer pace. The calibration on the speedometer is suspect, because the court doesn't know who calibrated it or what the person's qualifications were. Therefore, a reasonable doubt as to the speed obtained."

"2)   The officer's testimony is inherently unreliable. The officer testified that there are 3 miles between the two streets, that he paced for 2½ miles, that the highest speed he reached was 70 mph, that the greatest distance between the two vehicles was ¼ mile, and that the speed of the paced vehicle was constant.

All the facts cannot be true. At some time the officer had to close the ¼ mile distance and the 2½ mile pace, if you take into account the ½ mile pull-over. This could not have been true.

Our theory is that the paced vehicle was doing less than 70 mph, but to close the gap between the two vehicles, the officer was going faster than the paced vehicle. That's when he looked down at the speedometer that was reading 70 mph; and although the officer has proven he was doing 70 mph, the paced vehicle was doing less.

Thank you, Your Honor."

Step 12/13: Verdict/Sentence. True to the end, the judge just won't let himself, his D.A. and his cop be embarrassed (at least not in his court).

Judge: You are guilty—everyone goes that fast.

You: Your Honor, before sentencing, I would like to explain that I was only doing 63 mph, not 70 mph. I was going with the flow of traffic. I know that because my neighbor was traveling at the same time and he saw me get the ticket. I needed him to tell me the speed because my speedometer wasn't working. Finally, I didn't know it was a 55 mph zone.

You do get to say those things. They are not defenses, but they are mitigating factors in your case that may reduce your fine.

I gave you a "best case" fact scenario with a "worst case" result to make a point. You may pay some money and get some points on your license, *but you will feel good about yourself.*

That's what I mean about keeping it in perspective.

Example 2—The City Cop Radar Ticket

You know what they look like, but it seems that you never remember exactly where they are. "They" are, of course, those long stretches of road, often with a long gentle curve at the end. Along part of them is some significant obstruction, like a line of trees, a road burm, or of course the traditional road sign. Get the picture yet? We know these as "speed traps," but local police call them "cherry patches," because the "pickin' is so easy" when it comes to writing tickets.

Defending radar (the primary tool of speed traps) tickets is a lot different from defending the "pacing" speeding ticket that you just read about. To begin with, you *are* going to testify in this case.

Much of your defense will be based on an understanding of the basic terms. The violation is "Unsafe Speed," not "Exceeding the Maximum Speed Limit." The difference is that the prosecution has to show that your speed was "unsafe," and you can try to show that your speed, regardless of the posted "limit," was "safe."

The use of radar is a great advantage to you. It makes it easier for the cops to ticket you, but at trial there are more things they have to prove; therefore, more opportunity for you to allow them to lose it.

First, let's look at the charge against you.

Basic Speed Law

"No person shall drive a vehicle upon a highway at a speed greater than is reasonable or prudent, hav-

*ing due regard for weather, visibility, the traffic on
the surface and width of the highway, and in no
event at a speed which endangers the safety of persons or property."*

The exact wording is no doubt different in each jurisdiction, but the intent of these codes is always essentially the same. Safety is the guiding principle.

Look at it this way. If it is true that adverse weather
conditions such as fog can make driving at the posted
speed limit "unsafe," then it can also be true that the in-
version of such conditions could render driving in excess
of the speed limit "safe."

Back to the quoted law. Break it down into little sec-
tions, then make the prosecution prove each element of
the case.

1) *"No person SHALL . . ."* That's you, but the prosecution must prove that you were the one behind the
wheel. (Cop has to identify you as the driver.) **Defense: Maybe you weren't driving.**

2) *". . . drive a vehicle. . . ."* You have to be in a car,
motorcycle, truck, or RV, whatever. The cop, again,
has to establish a vehicle. **Defense: Usually the cop
has to personally observe you.**

3) *". . . upon a highway . . ."* You, in your car, have to
be on the highway, street or alley, and these facts
must be established by the prosecution. **Defense:
Maybe you were on a private dirt road.**

4) *". . . at a speed greater than is reasonable or prudent. . . ."* This is the essence of the case for the prosecution and you. The prosecution must establish that
your speed was unreasonable or imprudent. **Defense: Maybe the speed of your car was completely
reasonable or prudent.**

5) *". . . having due regard for weather, visibility, the traffic on, and the surface and width of, the highway . . ."* The prosecution must show the factors that establish the unreasonableness of the speed. **Defense: The weather was clear and dry, and there was no traffic (we'll deal with this later in the "Radar" section), with a good, wide street. Therefore, a reasonable speed was being observed.**

6) *". . . And in no event a speed which endangers the safety of person or property."* This is a kind of catch-all provision for the prosecution. **Defense: There was no one and nothing endangered.**

Note: *Nowhere does the statute refer to the Posted Speed Limit. But the cop will always put 45 mph in a posted 30. The posted speed creates a presumption (in some cases, an illusion) of what a safe speed is.*

Break down the law into its parts, and you can see there is a possibility of winning your case. More to the point, since the cop will have to testify to each of the elements, you're going to give the prosecution a real good chance to lose their case.

Remember, just like our first example, you have to win (allow them to lose) only one of the elements, and you win the case.

Now let's get into a "real world" example. I am going to cite an example based on a successful case that I tried recently. Put yourself in the defendant/attorney/ witness mode, and we pick up the trial at Step 5, the prosecution's case. Your "attorney" personality is taking furious notes and objecting to everything.

Step 5: The Prosecution's Case.

Your game plan: Make them prove every part of their case against you.

Officer Jones is sworn in and testifies:

Jones: I am employed by the City of Laguna Beach. I was on duty and in uniform, driving on a marked motorcycle on November 4, 1992. At approximately 10:30 a.m. on Laguna Canyon Road at Frontage I observed a 1989 Cadillac Seville, black in color . . .

You: OBJECTION. The officer seems to be reading from a document. (The citation.)

Judge: Officer, do you need the citation to testify?

Jones: No.

Judge: Please put it away and continue.

Jones: I saw the vehicle traveling eastbound on Laguna Canyon Road approaching my location. I visually estimated his speed at 55 mph. Traffic was medium; road dry; clear day. I then activated my hand-held Falcon 500 Radar Gun and pointed at the vehicle and obtained a reading of . . .

You: OBJECTION, foundation . . .

Judge: I'll overrule the objection at this time, subject to foundation being established.

Jones: I then pursued the vehicle and issued a citation to the driver for 54 mph in a 45 mph zone.

Judge: Any questions of this officer?

You: No questions.

D.A.:   The people rest, Your Honor.

Step 6: Motion for Dismissal. You make a motion for dismissal, based on:

1. Motion to strike officer's testimony—no foundation— for the use of Radar.

2. No identification of the driver of the vehicle.

3. Not showing that 54 mph was unsafe. A citation 54/45 is not evidence against me. Therefore, the officer's testimony that he cited me for 54 mph in a 45 mph shouldn't be used against me.

The judge denies all your motions and allows the cop to re-open his case. You object to this, and again, the Court overrules your objection.

Intent on proving the case himself now, the judge asks Officer Jones directly:

Judge: Who was driving the vehicle?

Jones: The defendant seated at the counsel's table was driving. (What a surprise!)

Judge: Officer, what is Foundation for the radar?

Jones: The Falcon 500 hand-held Radar unit was calibrated on 2–6–92.

You: OBJECTION—best evidence. (The document.)

Jones: I have it.

Officer Jones offers it into evidence as People's Exhibit #1.

You: OBJECTION, hearsay. The person who did the calibration is not present.

Jones: I have a certified copy of the calibration.

The judge overrules your objection and allows the certification in.

Jones: I tested the radar internally before and after each citation by pressing a test button that reads "888" if the unit is operating properly. And on this date it was operating properly. I also had an external check with a tuning fork . . .

You: OBJECTION.

The judge immediately overrules, but, hey, you're getting pretty good at this. Officer Jones continues.

Jones: . . . that I struck at the beginning of the shift and read 55 mph on a 55 mph tuning fork. I am qualified to use the radar because I have had eight hours of training from the factory.

Foundation met. (But see how many chances you gave them to screw up? Good going!)

In some states, the street where you got the ticket also has to qualify as not being a "speed trap." A Traffic Survey has to have been done on the street within the last five years.

Jones: That due to the area, a four-lane highway into a residential area, with a school two blocks away, a speed of 45 mph was safe and reasonable for the conditions, and in my opinion 54 mph was unsafe.

Judge: Any questions of the officer?

This time, you're not going to be so nice. So start off as if you are.

You: Thank you, yes, I do. Officer Jones, what color is your motorcycle?

Jones: It's blue and white.

You: Were you on duty for the main purpose of traffic
         enforcement?

Jones: Yes. (This is kind of obvious, but you have to get
         him to admit to it. Here's why:)

You: Motion to strike the officer's testimony on the ba-
         sis of illegally obtained evidence, based on non-
         conforming color of his motorcycle.

California Law states that a cop's "motorcycle must
be painted BLACK AND WHITE OR WHITE to legally
enforce the Vehicle Code section if he is on duty for the
Main or Exclusive purpose of enforcing the Vehicle
Code . . ." Back when you were researching the code violation, you should have checked this type of law out in
your state. Some laws really do protect citizens.
      YOU WIN!!! (I did.)
      Okay, but let's say the court doesn't buy it and de-
nies your motion. You keep going:

You: Officer, have you any formal training in deter-
         mining what a safe speed is?

Jones: No formal training.

You: How wide is the road at the location?

Jones: Two lanes in each direction.

You: Is there parking on the side of the road?

Jones: Yes, ah, I mean no. (This is the kind of detail he is
         not likely to have at hand; another area where your
         superior preparation gives you the upper hand.)

You: If "Yes," were there any cars parked to interfere
         with your radar gun?

This is a great cat and mouse game. He thinks you're setting him up as if there were lots of cars on the road, so he might have targeted the wrong car or gotten a bad reading. His testimony tries to counter that to eliminate all traffic so his radar unit is not affected by any outside interference. In fact, what you really want to show is that there is no traffic on the road, and a speed higher than the posted speed may be safe and reasonable. But Officer Jones's overconfidence is your best friend, so he answers your question:

Jones: No.

You: Did you use your RADAR to determine the speed of the vehicle?

Jones: Yes. (If "No," then 54 mph is suddenly an estimate, not a fact.)

You: Were there any cars in front of my vehicle?

Jones: No.

You: Any vehicle behind my vehicle?

Jones: No.

You: Any cars going in the opposite direction?

Jones: No.

You: Any bicycles in either direction? (By now, Officer Jones thinks he is really on to your "too-many-vehicles" game.)

Jones: No.

You: Any pedestrians in either direction?

Jones: No.

You: Nothing on the street to interfere with your radar reading, correct?

Jones: Right.

Thank you, Officer Jones. Now you move in for the kill.

You: Your estimate of 45 mph as a safe and reasonable speed was based on all your factors as to weather, road conditions, traffic and visibility, correct?

Jones: Yes.

You: You based 45 mph as safe on medium traffic, right? (Remember, your notes reminded you that he said "medium traffic" when he first got on the stand.)

Jones: Yes.

You: Would you consider no traffic in front, behind, or going in the opposite direction medium traffic?

Jones: No, er, yes. (For the second time, you got an "er/ah" answer out of him.)

Remember, though, you've got a judge who may be taking all of this a little personally, so keep up the pressure and make it easy for the judge to do the right thing.

You: Would you change your opinion as to what a safe and reasonable speed is if the traffic was light instead of medium?

Jones: No.

You: You would not consider traffic as a factor in estimating safe speed, officer?

Jones: No.

You: Officer, isn't there an open area north of your location?

Jones: Yes. (By now, he knows that you know, so he's not taking any chances, even though he doesn't clearly remember.)

You: Isn't it a fact that the first building is 50 feet south of your location?

Jones: Yes.

You: When you pointed your radar gun it was pointed north, correct?

Jones: Right.

You: Wasn't it a fact that the vehicle's speed was slowing?

Jones: I don't know.

You: Isn't it a fact that the school you mentioned is two blocks south of your location?

Jones: Right.

You: Isn't it true that there were no children on the street, as school had been in session for over 1½ hours?

Jones: True.

You: Given those conditions of light traffic in a rural area, would you revise your estimate of a safe speed?

Jones: Yes, no . . .

You: Officer Jones, what is the fastest speed you would consider safe under those conditions?

If he says 55 mph, you win. Don't ask any further questions. But just to keep the drama going, lets say he doesn't:

Jones: 50 mph, (he says, knowing that he got you for 54 mph).

You: Officer, would you say that is a conservative estimate?

Jones: Yes/No . . . (Getting him to answer at all is the key here.)

You: Nothing further, Your Honor.

D.A.:   PEOPLE REST (*Finally,* the D.A. thinks)

You: MOTION FOR DISMISSAL, insufficient . . .

Judge: DENIED.

Step 7: Defendant's Case. You will want to testify in this matter to establish that your speed was safe and reasonable under the circumstances. You have your diagram of the area leading into the city.

You want to be as consistent with the officer's testimony as possible. Your points of disagreement will stand out more if you agree on the meaningless details.

You: Your Honor, I am familiar with the area, as I drive it every day. As the road approaches the city limits it is two lanes in each direction. It is a rural area. There is a posted 55 mph zone approximately 2½ miles up the canyon.

The next sign is approximately 100 feet north of the officer's location. This sign indicates the speed is reduced to 45 mph.

As I approached the officer's location, I was traveling approximately 55 mph—Point "A" on the diagram. I took my foot off the accelerator and I saw the motorcycle cop get on his bike. The area is open farm

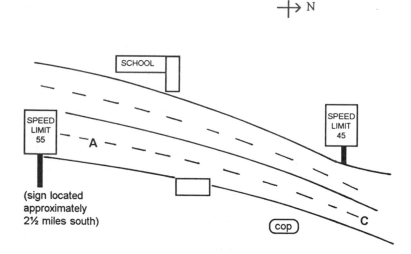

land on the right with no driveways or streets. On the left is a hillside. There was no traffic on the road that day, neither north nor south. The day was clear, the road was dry. There was no pedestrian traffic.

I started to slow down, and by the time I was even with the police motorcycle I was traveling at 45 mph. I saw the officer pull out directly behind me and activate his red light. We stopped approximately 100 yards south of the driveway that he was sitting in—Position "C".

I've been driving for over 12 years, and considered my speed down the canyon safe and reasonable. I was beginning to slow as the officer mounted his motorcycle.

I was traveling at a safe speed at all times.

You will now be cross-examined by the District Attorney or the Court.

DO NOT LET THE POLICE OFFICER ASK YOU ANY QUESTIONS. HE IS NOT AN ATTORNEY. "OBJECT" FOR THE RECORD.

Step 7B: Cross-Examination.

Remember, you're in control because you're better prepared than they are, so don't get intimidated. The D.A. doesn't have too much, so he may go "fishing." The best way to answer questions is to:

1) LISTEN carefully to the question.

2) Answer *only* the question asked. Don't volunteer information.

3) Keep your answers as short as possible. He may be fishing and not have anything to go on until you give him something.

4) Answer truthfully.

Mentally run a videotape of the incident. "Freeze" the tape at the questions asked and describe what is there.

D.A.: Where were you going?

You: I was going home.

D.A.: How fast were you going? (He's trying to get you to admit guilt.)

You: When? (You don't bite.)

D.A.: How fast were you going when you were coming down the canyon?

You: I was going approximately 55 mph.

D.A.: When the radar gun was pointed at you, how fast were you going?

You: I don't know when the radar gun was pointed at me.

D.A.: Did you see the officer before he pulled you over?

You: Yes.

D.A.: When did you see him first?

You: I saw the officer as he started to mount his motorcycle. I was approximately 200 yards north of his location.

D.A.: How fast were you going at that time?

You: I took my foot off the accelerator and was decelerating from 55 to 50 mph.

D.A.: What is the speed limit at that location?

You: At what location? (Make him explain himself. No one can get mad at you for asking to clarify a question.)

D.A.: Where you took your foot off the accelerator?

You: 55 mph.

D.A.: Does it change to 45 mph at some point?

You: Yes.

D.A.: Where?

You: Approximately 150 yards north of the officer's location. (He wanted you to get frustrated and angry, but your knowledge of the facts got the better of him here.)

D.A.: When you saw the officer mount the motorcycle, where were you?

You: Approximately 100 yards north of his location.

D.A.: So you had passed the 45 mph sign?

You: Yes.

D.A.: And after you passed the 45 mph sign, you were still traveling at 50 to 55 mph?

You: Yes.

D.A.: NOTHING FURTHER, YOUR HONOR!

The D.A. just thought he had won the case on your testimony by having you admit that after you passed the posted 45 mph sign, you were (by your own admission) traveling 50 to 55 mph.

However, you go on re-direct and say:

You: Your Honor, the nature of the roadway does not change until after you pass south of the officer's location.

You make a motion to introduce your diagram and/or pictures into evidence.

Step 11: Final Arguments. The D.A. will argue that the facts show that the visual observation of this highly trained officer was consistent with the radar unit that was calibrated and working properly and shows that the defendant (you) was traveling at a higher rate of speed than the posted 45—which creates a presumption of safe speed. Therefore, the court should find the defendant guilty.

You want to argue that the charge is "unsafe speed," not exceeding the posted 45 mph sign. Although the posted speed does create a presumption of what a safe speed is, the facts in the case would tend to support the contention that 50 or 55, if deceleration is occurring, may be a safe and reasonable speed. Based on the road, weather and traffic conditions on this particular occasion, the speed of 54 mph may be safe and reasonable.

Uncontradicted evidence shows that the vehicle was slowing; that the road goes from a 55 mph to a 45 mph zone at this location; that the terrain does not change until after the officer's location.

There is a tendency to go over every bit of evidence that was presented. However, the judge was also there during the testimony, so just tell why it is important to your case—don't retell the testimony itself.

The officer admitted that his estimate of 50 mph at that location, at that particular time, would be conservative. The testimony shows that 54 mph may have been safe and reasonable under the circumstances. Therefore, the Defendant is entitled to a Not Guilty verdict.

The D.A. will get the last argument before the judge. DO NOT really be concerned with what he says. You have done all you can do. Let it be.

Wait for the judge's decision, and if found GUILTY, ask about:

1) Traffic school.

2) Fine reduction from 54 mph in a 45 to 54 in a 50, per officer's testimony.

3) Mitigating factors (see example 1) of "You're such a nice guy," "you prepared so hard," etc.

Example 3—Judgment Cases

The next group of cases involves tickets that call the judgment of the driver into question. These alleged violations can include:

1) Failure to yield Right of Way,

2) Following too close,

3) Illegal lane change,

And the all-time favorite among cops,

4) Red light violations.

As they are some of the most difficult cases to win, we'll focus on red light violations. Because the police officer WILL testify consistent with "Guilty," he must state that when the light turned from yellow to red you were not in the intersection (and usually two to three car lengths behind the limit line). Your preparation will anticipate that testimony. You will need diagrams and light phasing, complete with the length of each light, etc.

Unless you got hit by a train trying to beat the signal, a red light violation is almost always an offense that is a judgment call. The light turns from green to yellow to red, and at some point your vehicle is legal when entering the intersection on the yellow, and illegal when entering the intersection after the light has turned red. In other words, passing through an intersection at one moment may be completely legal. Then, just a split second later, the exact same action becomes illegal.

Think you're stuck in a "your-word-against-the-cop's" trap? Think again. Same jerk judge, macho cop and surly prosecutor (D.A.); let's see how to handle them in judgment cases:

Step 1: Your case is called.

You: READY FOR TRIAL, YOUR HONOR.

The police officer isn't there, so the court dismisses the case. Hey, it does happen!

So maybe you weren't so lucky. He was hiding in the back. Officer Jones is sworn and testifies:

Jones: On May 5, 1993, at 6:30 p.m., I was on duty in uniform on routine patrol for the City of Wherever, in a marked Black and White patrol unit in the County of Whatever. I was approaching the intersection of First and Grand at the red light for eastbound First Street.

As a veteran of examples 1 & 2, you know what to do:

You: OBJECTION, YOUR HONOR, HE SEEMS TO BE READING FROM SOME NOTES.

Judge: Officer, please put your notes away.

Jones: I was in the #1 lane approaching Grand when I observed my light for eastbound traffic phase from red to green. I looked to my right and I noticed, er, . . . Your Honor, may I refer to my notes?

Court allows him to refresh his recollection. He continues.

Jones: I noticed a white Mustang northbound, approximately two to three car lengths behind the limit line, proceed through the intersection. I then entered the intersection, made a left-hand turn and pulled the subject's vehicle over. The subject then denied having run the light.

You: OBJECTION, hearsay. Only confessions or admissions can come into evidence. So if I said, "I ran the red," that would be admission.

Judge: Sustained.

Jones: I then issued the subject a citation for running a red light.

You: OBJECTION, relevance. What an officer issues a ticket for is irrelevant, since it is not fact.

Judge: Overruled.

D.A.: Nothing further.

Judge: Any questions of this officer?

Do you think you have it won? On what grounds? Don't ask any questions and see what happens.

You: NO QUESTIONS, YOUR HONOR.

D.A.: PEOPLE REST.

You were waiting for those words. Time for Step 6, Motion for Dismissal.

You: I would like to make a Motion for Dismissal on the grounds that the People's case is insufficient as it stands now, in that:

1) There has been no showing of the color of the light. The testimony of the officer was that the light changed from red to green; nothing as to what color the light was for northbound traffic.

2) There was no identification of the driver of the vehicle.

You're right and the dismissal should stand, but this IS traffic court, so let's assume the worst. This really ticks off the Court, and the judge allows the officer to re-open.

You: OBJECTION TO RE-OPENING for the record, Your Honor.

Judge: OVERRULED.

D.A.: Officer, who was the driver of the vehicle?

Jones: The defendant seated at counsel table.

D.A.: Officer, what color was the light for northbound traffic when the white Mustang entered the intersection?

Jones: Red.

Judge: THE MOTION FOR DISMISSAL IS OVER-RULED.

You: I would like to cross-examine the officer, then.

Judge: You had your opportunity to cross-examine the officer and declined. Proceed with your case.

About this time, you get a feeling you are not getting a fair trial, but keep going. You've got "RALFY" on your side.

You: The first witness I'd like to call is Officer Jones. Officer Jones, you understand that you are still under oath?

Sure, reminding him he's under oath sounds like an old Perry Mason trick. Well, it worked for him. It establishes control and puts the officer on the defensive.

You: Where were you when you first observed the white vehicle?

Jones: Approximately 200 feet west of Grand on First.

You: How fast were you traveling?

Jones: Approximately 35 mph.

You: What color was your light at that time?

Jones: Red.

You: How close were you to the light when it changed to green?

Jones: 150 feet.

You: What lane were you in?

Jones: Number 1, or fast lane.

You: What was your speed at that time?

Jones: 35 mph.

You: Was there any other traffic in front of you?

Jones: No.

You: Did you see any other traffic at that intersection?

Jones: I can't recall.

You: What lane was the white car in?

Jones: I can't recall.

You: Was there any other traffic northbound on Grand?

Jones: I can't recall.

You: What speed do you estimate the white vehicle at?

Jones: I don't know (or, 35 mph).

You: Where did you stop me?

Jones: I don't know.

You: When did you activate your overhead lights?

Jones: I don't recall.

The pattern of Officer Jones's behavior starts to emerge.

> You: Did I respond directly when you did activate your overhead lights?
>
> Jones: Yes.
>
> You: Isn't it a fact that it was when I was going east on 4th Street at McClay?
>
> Jones: Yes, er, no (pause). I don't know.

If Jones answers "Yes," you've got the facts you need to argue:

1) You responded directly to the lights, and

2) It was some four blocks away from the First and Grand intersection.

If "No," he has already testified that he doesn't know where he stopped you.

If he says "I don't know," your testimony will be the only evidence as to where the stop took place. This is important because you can back him up on his distance from the intersection response.

> You: Isn't it a fact that I was in the number 1 lane (fast lane)?
>
> Jones: I don't know.
>
> You: Isn't it a fact, officer, that there was another white car behind me in the number 2 lane (slow lane)?
>
> Jones: Yes/No/I don't know.

If "Yes," you've got your chance to argue he had mistaken your car for the other white car.

If "No," he's already testified he doesn't remember if there were other cars going north.

If "I don't know," your testimony will be the only evidence.

This line of questioning shows that the officer could have made an honest mistake (reasonable doubt).

On cross-examination you want to get as much of your evidence out as possible through the police officer. Ask him anything EXCEPT what color the light was in your direction.

You: The lights are hooded at Grand and First, correct?

Jones: Yes.

You: When your light turned green, you were 150 feet away from the intersection. Correct?

Jones: Yes.

You: You didn't actually see the light for northbound Grand Avenue, did you?

Jones: No, but . . .

You: OBJECTION, YOUR HONOR, NON-RESPON-SIVE after the word "No."

Judge: I'll allow him to answer.

Jones: No, but I could see my light turn green.

You: You made a left turn, correct?

Jones: Yes.

You: Was there any traffic coming the other way?

Jones: No.

You: Did you see any traffic pass me?

Jones: No.

You: Did you see any other vehicle on the road?

Jones: No.

You: Did you ever lose sight of the vehicle that went through the intersection?

Jones: No.

You: Isn't it a fact that my vehicle turned right on 4th Street?

Jones: Yes.

You: How far away were you when I turned right on 4th Street?

Jones: 300 feet.

You: How many streets go to the right between 1st and 4th?

Jones: I don't recall.

You: Isn't it a fact that there are two streets between 1st and 4th?

Jones: Yes, but neither has a signal.

You: Did you see the white vehicle that turned right on 2nd Street?

Technically, this is an objectionable question because it assumes facts not in evidence. But the D.A. may not be awake.

Jones: There wasn't one./I didn't see it.

"There wasn't one." He's already testified he doesn't know if there was other traffic going northbound.

"I didn't see it." You got what you need, because you can testify the white car turned right on 2nd Street.

You can do this all day long! First, ask a general question that he'll answer with "I don't know" or "I can't recall," then zero in on a specific question that will help your case.

> You: Officer, then you did lose sight of my vehicle momentarily?
>
> Jones: Just for a second.
>
> You: OBJECTION, YOUR HONOR, NON-RESPONSIVE. CALLS FOR A "YES" or "NO" ANSWER.
>
> Judge: (to Jones) Just answer the question "Yes" or "No."
>
> Jones: Yes, but just for a second.
>
> You: OBJECTION NON-RESPONSIVE AFTER THE WORD "YES." MOTION TO STRIKE.
>
> Judge: OVERRULED.

About now, you can expect a response from the judge something like this:

> Judge: And hurry up your case. You're taking too much time.

The judge does have the right to control the courtroom. But he does not have the right to deny you a fair trial. Move it along, but have the Court Clerk note the judge's comments for the record.

Okay, you've worked hard on your preparation, you've figured out that they can't throw you in jail for being prepared, and your confidence is high. Given that there's still a good chance you're going to lose the case to "blind justice" anyway, why not extract some of your own revenge . . . perfectly legal. Your "weapons" are your preparation and the cop's lack of it. Here's a sample:

You: So, you testified earlier that you "NEVER LOST
        SIGHT OF THE VEHICLE THAT WENT
        THROUGH THE INTERSECTION." Is that still
        your testimony, Officer Jones?

Jones: Yes, ah, no. (You've trapped him either way.)

You: You did lose sight of the vehicle, didn't you?

Jones: Yes, but . . . (You interrupt him.)

You: You testified that you were 150 feet away from the
        intersection in the #1 eastbound lane, correct?

At this point, Jones is looking for help anywhere he
can get it.

Jones: Your Honor, I already testified to that.

You: Your Honor, please direct the witness to answer
        the question.

Judge: Just answer the question, Officer.

Jones: Yes.

You: These traffic lights are hooded, right?

Jones: Yes.

You: Isn't it a fact that you could not see the color of the
        light for the northbound or southbound traffic?

Jones has had it now.

Jones: Your Honor . . .

So has the judge.

Judge: Just answer the question. It's about lunch time.

Jones: Yes.

You: So when you testified that the light was RED, you didn't actually see the north/southbound light, did you, Officer?

Jones: No.

BE NICE TO THE GUY—HE'S HAD ENOUGH.

You've caught Officer Jones twice in a lie on the stand under oath. Now, in your best Perry Mason imitation, you say with a disgusted tone:

You: NOTHING FURTHER OF THIS WITNESS, YOUR HONOR.

Step 9: Rebuttal Witness.

Judge (to D.A.):   Re-direct.

On friendlier turf, Jones tries to counter-punch.

Jones: Your Honor, I'd like to add that what I meant was I saw the red GLOW from the hood of the light.

Step 10: Re-Cross-Examination. Jones just had to get the last shot in, but you were ready for it:

You: So you DID see the red light?

Jones: No—just the glow.

You: Officer, it was May 5, correct?

Jones: Yes.

You: It was at 6:30 p.m., correct?

Jones: Yes.

You: It was Daylight Saving Time, correct?

Jones: Yes.

By now, even Jones has got this figured out, but there's nothing he can do about it.

You: It was still light out, correct?

Jones: It was sunset.

You: Did you have your headlights on?

Jones: No. (If he says "yes," ask him if he always has his lights on when the car isn't running.)

You: So it was light enough not to need headlights?

Jones: Right.

You: There was no "glow" you could see in the hood of the light, was there?

Jones: Yes, I could see a faint glow.

It seems like you're stuck here, back in the "his-word-against-yours" mode. Look how you escape:

You: In fact, Officer, you said that when you saw your light turn green, you looked to your right and saw the white vehicle?

Jones: Yes.

You: When you were looking to your right, is that when you noticed the "red glow" on the hooded light?

Jones: Yes.

You: When you testified to seeing the "red glow", that is the light you meant, right?

Jones: Yes.

You: Isn't it a fact that that light is for SOUTHBOUND traffic on Grand Avenue?

Jones: Yes.

You: So you never saw the "glow" from the hooded light for northbound; isn't that true, Officer?

Jones: Yes.

Jones has been nailed again (didn't it feel great)! In a really disgusted tone, you repeat:

You: Nothing further, Your Honor.

Re-re-direct. Jones hasn't given in yet (they never do):

Jones: Your Honor, I went immediately back and checked the phasing of the lights, and they were all working properly.

Good move on Jones's part. He's fast on his feet.

                 So when the southbound light is red, so it is for northbound traffic. Also, when eastbound 1st Street has a green light, north and south have a red light. Also, the relay switches that control the intersection won't . . .

You: OBJECTION—no foundation for giving an expert opinion.

Judge: Officer, are you qualified to testify as an expert in the field of traffic engineering?

Jones: No.

Judge: Objection sustained. We'll break for lunch; be back at 2:30 p.m.

Judges are into long lunches.

Judge: Anything further for the defense?

You: Yes, a few more questions of the officer. Officer, you said you went back and checked the phasing of the light?

Jones: Yes.

You: Did you do that immediately after issuing the citation to me?

Jones: Yes.

You: We all noticed earlier that you took notes in this case, right?

Jones: Yes.

You: When did you make those notes?

Jones: Right after issuing the citation.

You: How long did it take you to write down the notes?

Jones: About five minutes.

The Judge is now impatient.

Judge: I don't see the relevancy of this line of questions, and it is beyond the scope of Re-Re-Direct.

You: Offer of Proof, Your Honor. That he testified he went back to check the phasing of the light immediately after issuing the citation. These questions tend to show he did not go IMMEDIATELY back . . .

Judge: O.K., I'll allow only a little more.

Remember, you took better notes than he did at the time of the ticket. Now is the time to use them.

You: Isn't it a fact, officer, that after you wrote the ticket, then took five minutes to write the notes, you then proceeded down 4th Street and over the Freeway and entered the On Ramp for northbound I–5?

Jones: I don't recall. (Got him again!)

You: NOTHING FURTHER, YOUR HONOR.

D.A.:   PEOPLE REST.

You: Motion for dismissal on insufficiency of evidence.

Judge: Motion granted. Case dismissed.

Only kidding! But it is possible.

Step 7: Defendant's Case. You get to explain your case in a narrative, without interruption, except by the Court:

You: Your Honor, on the day in question, I was going to the baseball game that starts at 7:35 p.m. (in other words, you're a nice guy who was *not* in a hurry). I was in the fast lane. Your Honor, I have a diagram of the area I would like to mark for identification.

Bailiff: Marked as Defendant's #1.

Go to the diagram and tell your story—one frame at a time.

You: As I proceeded north on Grand Avenue, I was traveling at approximately 30 to 35 mph. As I approached the intersection of 1st and Grand, I noticed the light was green for my direction. As

I got to within 50 to 75 feet of the intersection, the light phased green to yellow.

Special Tip:

Traveling at 30 to 35 mph, you can estimate that you travel 1½ times as many feet per second as mph (30 mph × 1½ = 45 feet per second; 35 mph × 1½ = 52.5 feet per second, etc.).

Normally a yellow light for an intersection lasts one second for each 10 mph posted; so a 30 mph posted street will have a three-second yellow light. A 40 mph posted street will have a four-second yellow, and so on.

You: I made a judgment decision that I could not safely stop at the limit line. I noticed to my right in the slow lane a car behind me that was a white Toyota Camry traveling at between 40 to 45 mph. As I entered the intersection the light was yellow and the Toyota was still behind me. I saw the light phase from yellow to red as I was approaching the north limit line.

The white Toyota passed me first north of the intersection of 1st and Grand and turned right on 2nd Street. As I approached 3rd Street, I saw the police officer make a left turn from 1st to northbound Grand. I moved over to the right lane and made a right turn on 4th Street. I saw the officer make a right turn on 4th and half way down the block he turned on his red light. I pulled over to the side, and he issued me a citation. I told him I didn't run a red light and was trying to explain what happened when he said he didn't want to hear about it and told me to "tell it to the Judge."

It's about ¼ mile between 1st Street and 4th Street and about ⅛ mile between Grand and 4th, where the officer pulled me over at McClay Street.

I couldn't believe he gave me a ticket. I read in a book not to argue with the officer. So I told him I didn't run the light and kept quiet. I was quite upset, so I pulled over into a parking lot and read the ticket over. As I was seated there I noticed the officer making notes.

I waited, trying to remember exactly what happened. I was there about two to three minutes, and I started to pull out of the driveway and noticed the officer starting to move. I waited for the officer to go in front of me, because I didn't want another ticket. He went down 4th Street towards the freeway and I followed.

He made the light at the freeway entrance (on the yellow) for northbound I–5. I waited at the red. At the time I didn't think anything of it, but the officer didn't go immediately back to check the intersection. I know that for a fact.

I would like to introduce Exhibit "A" into evidence.

Judge: Nothing further from the defense?

You: No, Your Honor.

Here's a twist you might see. The cop decides that he wants to try his hand at playing attorney.

Jones: I'd like to ask him some questions, Your Honor.

You: OBJECTION, Your Honor. He is not an attorney, and he does not represent the People.

Judge: I'll allow it. We don't have a District Attorney here and he seems to know what he's doing. I just want to get this over with. OBJECTION OVERRULED. GO AHEAD OFFICER, YOU MAY ASK QUESTIONS.

Jones: Did you see the light turn from green to yellow?

You: Yes.

Jones: Did you see the light turn from yellow to red?

You: Yes.

Jones: Did you tell me about this white car at the time I issued you the ticket?

You: No.

He says in an equally disgusted voice,

Jones: Nothing further for this witness, Your Honor.

Judge: Anything further?

You: Yes. I saw the light change from green to yellow prior to entering the intersection. I entered the intersection on the yellow and was almost all the way through when it changed to red.

          I didn't tell the officer about the other car because I was told not to argue with the officer.

STEP 11: Final Argument. First of all, object if the cop tries to argue the case. For your part, the first thing you want to tell the court is that you are NOT arguing that the light was defective and that somehow there were two green lights at the same time. But you should point out to the Court that the officer seems to be making up facts, such as "I immediately went back and checked the phasing," to support his position.

You should bring out to the court that this is a credibility issue, and that based on the criteria given, that you had the better opportunity to observe the color and phasing of the light. You were looking at it. The officer was seeing the reflection in the hood of the light (or lying). You have a better memory of the facts—you remember details of the incident where the officer "can't recall" whether he saw the white Toyota that turned right on 2nd Street. The officer could have mistaken your car for that one. The officer did lose sight of the vehicle for a moment. At best, the officer is making a mistake as to the identity of the vehicle; at worst, the officer is lying under oath.

The charge is entering into an intersection against a solid red, circular light. There is direct testimony that the light was yellow when you entered the intersection. Close with, "Your Honor, for the above reasons, you should find the defendant NOT GUILTY."

The officer jumps up and states that you ran the red light.

Again, you say, "Object—not an attorney."

The Court asks if there is anything further, and you want to keep talking, but you don't. The Court finds the defendant "Guilty, as charged."

> You: Can I attend traffic school instead of paying the fine?
>
> Judge: No. Can you pay the fine today?
>
> You: Yes, Your Honor.

I told you this is a hard type of case to win. You had fun and got the officer to admit he lied under oath—not a bad day. If you're really into it, you also have some possible appealable issues in the case, but for now, pay the fine and get on with life.

Example 4—Sign Cases

No, don't listen to your older brother. This section is not about being illegal because you're an Aries. The final group of cases is about those signs that *prohibit* you from doing something:

- STOP
- NO LEFT TURN
- NO U-TURN
- YIELD, etc.

Or signs that *require* you to do something:

- RIGHT LANE MUST TURN RIGHT
- RIGHT LANE MUST EXIT
- LEFT TURN ONLY
- NO RIGHT ON RED
- NO CROSSING OVER DOUBLE YELLOW LINES, etc.

As in every case, use "RALFY" to focus on the result you want, then find the issues in your case that will get you to "Not Guilty":

1)   Did you have adequate notice of the violation?

2)   Did you violate the restriction placed on the sign?

Here's a typical scenario for "sign" tickets that I see all the time. You're in a new town and you're running late for your 4 p.m. appointment. You're unfamiliar with the streets. Here's a thirty-second snapshot of a ruined day:

1. Working from the directions that your daughter wrote on the back of the phone bill, you look for the street sign.

2. Finally (her directions were three blocks off), you see the street.

3. Elated, you make a quick lane change because you couldn't see the street sign until you were right in front of it.

4. But even under pressure, you're a good driver, so you quickly glance and turn on your blinker.

5. On the yellow light, you make your left turn.

6. Next thing you know, you see a red light behind you and the cop pulls you over.

Having read this book prior to getting this ticket, you try to remain calm. Nice try with the head game, because instead, you're furious inside, knowing you will miss the meeting now. The cop asks for your driver's license and registration; takes them from you; goes back to the patrol unit; calls on the radio; and writes something down. All the while you're trying to rationalize that:

1. The meeting really wasn't that important.

2. They might buy this traffic ticket excuse (Try to recall whether or not you used that excuse before when you really didn't get one.)

Finally, the cop walks back up and smugly asks, "Do you know why I pulled you over?"
(You think, "Yes, it's because you're a jerk!")
But you say, "No, Officer."
The cop says you made a left turn back there.
(You think, "Da-huh! I'll bet you get the 'Investigator of the Year' award for that little gem, bucko!")

But you say, "So?"

He points to the sign that says, "No Left Turn between 4 and 6 p.m. Except Sundays and Holidays."

(You think, "Oh, you mean that 18″ × 24″ sign that I was 45 feet away from. The one next to the "No Truck Route" sign, above the "1 Hour Parking, Except on Tuesdays and Saturdays" sign, below the "Left Turn Only" sign, across from the "35 MPH Speed Limit, Except When School Children Present" sign, just ahead of the "Route 6A South," "Route 6A North/Route 89 West," and "I–10 This Way" signs, and right behind the "Rotary Club International, Meets every Third Tuesday in the Masonic Hall" sign. That one, Officer Jerk?")

But you say, "Oh."

This REALLY gets to you. But you pull on the advice from the book and you are not going to try the case out on the street. The cop asks you to sign the ticket, and adds, "Have a nice day."

Okay, so don't get mad, get even. You go into action even before he has left you.

You ask that the case be transferred to the county seat. He looks at you and says, "This IS the county seat."

Hey, you're new in town; how were you to know where the county seat was? Good try, at least you were thinking.

He issues the citation, you look at it and notice that he wrote "2–15–93" in the date section, and "1610 hrs." in the time slot. You ask him, "What's 1610?"

He says, "Military time for 4:10 p.m. That's the time I issued the citation."

You look down at your rental car digital clock and it says 4:05 pm. You're really super pissed, but don't say anything.

You go on with life and enter the parking garage one block away, and go to your boring meeting with your publisher. You don't need to be here to listen to another schedule being made up. You're still upset about your ticket. You pull out your garage ticket and it shows 1607 hrs. Aha! You now know that is 4:07 p.m. in the military.

Hey, wait a minute (or 3!), that can't be right. According to Officer Asshole, I was getting a ticket at 4:10 p.m.

After the meeting you go down and ask the attendant about the stamp. He tells you that there is a five minute grace period on all tickets, so the time would actually be 4:12 p.m., or 1612. You don't know now as you drive back to the hotel and listen to the news station and they say the time is exactly 6:00 p.m., and you notice the rental car clock is perfectly accurate.

Maybe you've got a case, but, hey, it's a long way away and you don't need the hassle. But after reading this book you know that you still have options:

1) You could go to traffic school, but it's in another state, and 8 hours of your time is too much.

2) You can have a Trial by Declaration; write all this out for the judge—surely he/she would understand.

3) You'll be back here in about three months. You could set it down for arraignment and trial on the same day.

The next day you go back through the intersection and you see the sign on the light pole:

> *NO LEFT TURN*
> *4 to 6 p.m.*
> *Except Sun. & Hol.*

But, with your anger and sarcasm under control, you notice in detail that there are also many other signs, control devices and other symbols that you are expected to recognize and respond to:

NO PARKING

NO U-TURN

RIGHT LANE MUST TURN RIGHT

RED LIGHTS

RED CURB

BIKE LANE

ROAD CLEANING PARKING RULES

etc.

Finally, you count 46 directional or prohibitive in-dications at the intersection. You make a sketch of the area and the signs.

Oh, yes; you also notice that the sign you suppos-edly violated was partially obscured by graffiti sprayed on by someone named "LOCO." Yes, the sign is there, but would it give reasonable notice to the driver? You decide to fight it.

Back home, you wait for a while and receive a "Courtesy Notice". (Don't you just love the way the gov-ernment likes to soften the blow?) You send in the money (post bail) and request the arraignment and trial be set for May 13, 1993, in the night court or in the afternoon of the same day. They write back and say that your "arraign-ment and trial" is set for May 14, 1993, at 8:30 a.m. in Division 208. You can live with it.

You schedule the rest of your trip around this court date, allowing plenty of extra time.

You show up. You've got two days to collect more evidence and take your pictures (if you didn't get them the first time). You've also brought your video camera. You get the same kind of car, but the clock doesn't work. You drive the same road, but it's now a one-way street.

You look for the same sign, but it's gone. The only thing that is the same is that "LOCO" can still spray paint in the dark.

Your case has just gone down the tubes. All this great evidence you were going to present—GONE. Right?

No way!. You may not have all the evidence you wanted, but you've got most of it. You have your

- Parking lot ticket

- Sketch

- Copy of the ticket with the error on it

- Own testimony

That will be good enough, because you can't worry about what you don't have. The meetings are great; they decide to publish your book on schedule. One reason is "RALFY." You used the same basic principles to sell the book as you are going to use to "sell" the judge. Work backwards from the results you want.

The morning of the trial you're getting cold feet. A prosecutor, Ms. Holmes, is there. "What the heck is a prosecutor doing on my case?" you wonder nervously. "This is just a little traffic ticket."

Relax. Ms. Holmes was assigned to work that day in court long before you showed up. And even if she is there for you, that may give you a tip that they know they need the help.

The court clerk calls out "The People of the State of Chicago vs. John Smith." People in Chicago think it's a state—I guess they think they got a right. It's a Cubs/ White Sox thing, I think.

Remember, at this point, the prosecutor's job is to talk as many people as she can out of going to trial. So she will talk to all the defendants, telling them that the officers have been subpoenaed, and that most of the time the judge believes the officer, and that the judge has heard it all before. But, she, as a prosecutor, will be willing to discuss your case with you to try and settle it without the "hassle" of going to trial. As you sit there you can see she is being fair, listening to the stories and shaking hands. You don't want to go to trial and look like a fool, so you think, "Why not play 'Let's Make a Deal' with her?"

By now you know that the prosecutor is not your friend. Her job is to convict you. The announcement is made that anyone wishing to talk with the prosecutor may do so out in the hall. You want to remain cool, but you're scared as you and a number of defendants file out. When it's your turn she says, "Tell me about your case. How can I help you?" With a few pleasant exchanges and then her subtle help, you're probably also getting nervous about what you don't have:

- I should have subpoenaed the Parking Lot attendant,

- Or at least gotten the City Engineer to verify the fact that the road has changed,

- Or looked up the law on how many signs could be posted at a given intersection (even though there is no such law).

Your mind screams "Plead Guilty" to anything, as long as they don't throw you in jail.

Okay, so you kind of want to tell her everything. First, you ask, "If you believe me, do you have the authority to dismiss the case?"

She says, "No." If she does say "Yes," be very careful. Remember, her job isn't to judge the facts, and why would she believe you if she hasn't heard what the cop has to say? You don't want to give her any information about the case for fear she will use it against you in trial or prepare the officer to negate a particular point. She's not there to help you. So, comfortable that you are in control, you are always willing to listen to what the other side has to say.

Let's say she offers to cut the fine in half from $108 to $54. You've just gotten a ½-price sale on justice and brought the system to its knees. You've won. Take it and get the hell out of there.

But have they offered you anything, really? If not for the pressure of the courtroom corridor, would you have taken this deal? Is this in your best interest? It's not the money. You've already spent the extra $54 on hotel rooms and rental cars for the extra day you've spent in town.

No, reject the offer, even as reasonable as she seems. She may come back with a veiled threat that the fine COULD go up after trial if you lose. That is possible, but the fine COULD also go down after trial. What she won't say, of course, is that the fine could go away altogether with a "Not Guilty" verdict.

She then offers you traffic school. As she so condescendingly explains, this will keep the ticket off your record and the case will be dismissed after completion. "Now how much fairer can she get," you think. She has just offered to dismiss the case if you're only smart enough to take it.

If you thought about this option at the beginning of the case and it was what you wanted then, you should have taken it then. If you rejected it at the beginning, you should reject it now. You thank her nicely, then firmly explain that you want your trial.

Now she tries to reason with you that she is a trained professional and a trial attorney; that the court won't give you any consideration because you don't know courtroom procedure or Rules of Evidence; and that you're assuming responsibility for the entire presentation of your case. So she suggests reasonably that she will grant you a continuance so you can retain an attorney of your own, if you really want to go through with it (isn't it great how the legal system feeds itself at your expense?).

Now you might think this is the first thing she has said that makes sense. You can hire an attorney, subpoena the parking lot attendant, and get the city engineer. Maybe the attorney can even get "LOCO" to come and testify.

KEEP THIS IN PERSPECTIVE. It's only $108 and one point on the driving record and insurance. All those things above would be good (except for LOCO), but you've already wasted enough time and energy on this case.

Thank her for her concern about your well-being, but respectfully decline and again pronounce that you want your trial without discussing the facts with her.

You go back inside the courtroom in a cold sweat. "Hey," you think, "if I left right now, I could catch the 11:20 a.m. flight home if I hurried." The court would call your case, no one would answer, the bail would be forfeited, and you wouldn't get embarrassed by the prosecutor. Sure, that's an option, but ask yourself two important questions:

1. What did she *really* say that was any different from what you expected her to say?

2. Maybe you didn't prepare a perfect case, but you *did* prepare a damn good one. So did you go through all that preparation just to walk out at the last minute?

Take these two questions to heart and you'll be a "winner" long after this trial is a faded memory.

So hang tough, you've earned it!

The judge finally calls your case, "People of the State of Chicago v. John Smith." Here we go again. Just like you practiced.

> You: Ready for trial, Your Honor.
>
> Holmes: The People state that they are having difficulty locating a witness, as the officer is off duty, and the prosecution requests a continuance in this matter.

You knew she didn't have her witness!

The Court looks at you and asks if you have any objections? Da-hah! You're going to say exactly what he didn't want to hear.

> You: Yes, your honor. I do object to a continuance because I'm from out of town and had to arrange my schedule to be here today, and it would be very inconvenient for me to come here again. Also, the prosecution gave neither me or the court any notice that they would be requesting a continuance, as required under section 1150 of the Penal Code.

"Whoa!", thinks the judge, "where did that come from, this guy's not an attorney?" But before you get too smug, be sure you check the right code reference for your jurisdiction.

The Court looks down at you and says to the prosecution:

> Judge: Motion to continue denied, but I will put the case at the end of the calendar and if your witness is not here, I will dismiss the case.

That's the first positive thing you've heard all day. The bad news is that you're going to be sitting until all the other cases have been heard.

Take this opportunity to practice your trial skills. During direct examination, just think where you would object.

What are the best questions for cross-examination?

What facts will be needed by the defense?

What are the questions the Prosecutor will ask?

How would you argue the case at the end of the trial?

What will the Judge sentence you to?

What would you do differently?

How many defendants convict themselves during trial?

If you get nervous, go take a walk. Or do that office or school work that you had planned on. Do those things that will help lower the anxiety of the situation. KEEP A PERSPECTIVE!

You come back from lunch at a little restaurant called "Loco's." Hmmmm? The cop is here now, seated in the rear of the courtroom. He doesn't seem to recognize you as you enter. And since there are only three of you in the courtroom this seems strange to you. Maybe he doesn't recognize you; maybe he forgot, but how could he when this is such a memorable event?

Finally, the judge takes the bench at 1420 hours—that's right, 2:20 p.m.—and he calls your case.

Judge:　　People of the state of Chicago v. John Smith.

The Prosecution announces "Ready," and you announce "Ready, Your Honor."

Then Officer Jones (him again!) is sworn and testifies that:

Jones:　　. . . I can't recall this ticket at all and have no independent recollection of the events.

You win . . . maybe. Ms. Holmes won't give up that easily after you made that sexist remark. She will try to make four distinct points:

Holmes: Officer Jones, did you write the ticket? (Point 1.)

Jones: Yes.

Holmes: At the time of the occurrence? (Point 2.)

Jones: Yes.

Holmes: And the statements were true when you wrote them down? (Point 3.)

Jones: True.

Holmes: And you have the notes in court today? (Point 4.)

Jones: True.

The prosecution then asks that the evidence be introduced over the hearsay objection based on PAST REC-OLLECTION RECORDED. At least she's giving you enough credit to anticipate your objection!

You: OBJECTION, Your Honor.

Judge: OVERRULED. The officer can now only testify from the citation itself.

She then gives Officer Jones a free rein to tell his story.

Jones: I issued this citation on February 15, 1993, at approximately 1610 hours for the violation . . .

Remember your training. He's about to accuse you, so you're on him:

You: OBJECTION.

Judge: OVERRULED. Continue.

Jones: . . . of disobeying a posted sign.

He looks on the back of the ticket.

Jones: The violation occurred on Wacker and Rush, making a left turn between the hours of 4:00 p.m. and 6:00 p.m.

Holmes: Do you see the driver of the vehicle in the courtroom today?

Jones: Yes.

Holmes: Would you point that person out for the court?

Jones: The gentleman seated at the counsel table wearing a black coat.

You: Objection, Your Honor, it's navy blue.

Judge: Granted.

You were just practicing.

Holmes: Nothing further, Your Honor. The People rest.

You: Motion for dismissal, Your Honor, on the grounds they have not established 1) jurisdiction of the court, 2) that the person qualifies as a proper party to issue a citation, 3) and that . . .

Judge: Motion denied.

Damn! Don't get discouraged, and don't forget that you only have to win once. The judge allows you to cross-examine:

You:	Officer Jones, is everything true and correct on the citation?
Jones:	Yes.
You:	Is it correct you have NO INDEPENDENT RECOLLECTION of the events of February 15, 1993?
Jones:	True.
You:	You can't remember what kind of car was involved?
Jones:	Not without looking at the ticket.
You:	Does the ticket refresh your recollection?
Jones:	No, but I would not have written it down if it weren't true.
You:	So you don't know what kind of car?
Holmes:	Objection. Asked and answered.
Judge:	Sustained. Move on.
You:	Do you remember me from that day?
Jones:	No, not really.
You:	But Officer Jones, you just identified me as the driver? (You ask rhetorically.)
Jones:	Yes.
You:	How can you be sure I was the driver of the vehicle?
Holmes:	OBJECTION, argumentative.
Judge:	SUSTAINED. You're taking too much time. Move the case along.

Ain't that choice! The System has wasted six hours of your time, but you take five minutes of its time, and it's you who are accused of wasting time. Don't forget, you are in the process of embarrassing them in front of a bunch of other people like you who didn't read this book. But you're cool:

You:	Yes, Your Honor. Officer, when do you put the time down on the citation?
Jones:	When I give it.

Make sure that you pin the officer down exactly. This will be important later.

You:	You mean that you write the time down when you issue the citation?
Jones:	Yes.
You:	Do you recall running a check on my license that day?
Jones:	No, but I usually do.
You:	Do you recall taking about five minutes to issue the citation?
Jones:	That sounds about right.
You:	How do you determine the time on the ticket?
Jones:	I look at my watch. (Jones looks at you like you're an idiot.)
You:	And your watch said 1610 hours?
Jones:	No. It said 4:10 p.m.
You:	What time does it say right now?
Jones:	2:40 p.m.
You:	Let the record reflect that the time on the courtroom clock reads 2:35 p.m.

Judge: The record will reflect 2:35 p.m.

Holmes: Objection, Your Honor, relevancy?

Jones: I can explain the difference.

Judge: Please.

Jones: I set my watch five minutes fast.

You: Thank you. What does the sign actually say?

Jones: "No left turn 4 to 6 p.m."

You: That's it?

Jones: Yes.

You: Doesn't it also say "except Sundays & Holidays?"

Jones: Yes, I think it does.

Score another point for you and "RALFY."

You: February 15, wasn't that President's Day—a holiday?

Jones: We didn't get the day off. (He's a little sarcastic, now. Remember, that's what they wanted to do to you.)

Jones: But it is a holiday, correct?

You: For some.

You have enough to argue right now, but you could go farther.

Jones: So only people who have the day off can turn left on holidays, right?

Holmes: Objection, argumentative.

Judge: OVERRULED. (The places where you find respect in these things can sometimes surprise you.)

Jones: No, only on state-recognized holidays.

You: Who is Loco?

Now he's both frustrated and confused!

Jones: That the restaurant down on the corner?

You: No, I mean on the street signs. There is a name "LOCO" spray painted on the signs. Who is that?

Jones: I don't know, but when I catch him . . .

You: Then you recognize that he . . .

The prosecutor is confused, too.

Holmes: Objection—relevancy.

Judge: Sustained. Move on.

You: But . . .

Judge: Move on, (he says more sternly).

You just get to the same place from a different direction.

You: At the time you wrote this ticket, isn't it a fact that the "NO LEFT TURN" sign had the letters LOCO sprayed over it?

Jones: Maybe, I don't remember.

You: How many signs were at the location of Wacker and Rush?

Jones: I don't know.

You: Isn't it a fact that there were 47 different infor-
          mational signs or signals at that corner?

Jones: I don't know.

You: Where is the "NO LEFT TURN" sign posted?

Jones: I don't recall.

You: Isn't it a fact that the sign was posted on the far
          left signal light pole between a "NO
          U-TURN" and a "NO PARKING" sign?

Jones: I don't recall.

You: How big was the sign?

Jones: I don't know—standard.

You: About 18 inches by 24 inches?

Jones: Yeah, I guess.

You: How big were the "Truck Route" signs?

Holmes: Objection—assumes facts not in evidence.

Judge: Sustained.

See how you easily move on.

You: Is the "NO LEFT TURN" sign bigger or smaller
          than the other signs posted on the pole?

Jones: They're all about the same size.

You: Nothing further, Your Honor.

Judge: Any re-direct by the People?

Holmes: No, the People Rest.

You: Motion for dismissal.

Judge: Denied. Is there any affirmative defense?

You get sworn in and testify in your "witness" mode:

You: I was driving down Wacker towards Rush, and
            I didn't know if I would be turning right or left
            on Rush so I was in the middle lane. I had a 4
            o'clock appointment at the publisher's and
            didn't want to be late. As I approached the in-
            tersection I saw the lovely building on the left.
            I moved over to the left lane, signaled and
            made my turn on the yellow light. The inter-
            section is very confusing because it is con-
            gested with numerous signs and lights.

            The officer pulled me over and asked for my li-
            cense and registration, which I gave to him. He
            walks back to his car, sits in there for quite a
            while, comes back out and tells me he is writing
            me a ticket for "No Left Turn." I look at the ticket
            and it says 1610 in the time slot. I ask him and
            he tells me that it is 4:10 p.m. civilian time.
            That's when I look at my clock in the rental car,
            and it says 4:05. I don't say anything because I
            didn't see the sign and the officer didn't explain
            that it was "No Left Turn" between 4 and 6 pm.
            I sign the ticket and go to the meeting.

Holmes: Objection.

Judge: Overruled. Continue.

You: I pull the ticket out and it says "No Left Turn
            between 4 and 6." I then pull out my garage
            parking receipt that I have here, and would
            like to mark for identification as Defendant Ex-
            hibit #1. The parking garage ticket is time
            stamped 4:07 pm.

Holmes: Objection, hearsay and relevancy.

Judge: Sustained.

You: But, Your Honor . . .

Judge: Move on.

Because you think this is a very important piece of evidence, make an "Offer of Proof" showing that this is relevant because it establishes the time of the occurrence. The Court agrees with you that it is relevant, but since it is 'Hearsay', the Court won't allow it unless foundation is shown. You should have subpoenaed the Parking Lot Attendant. DON'T WORRY. It would have been nice, but you have more evidence on that issue. It's important to stay focused on your ultimate result ("Not Guilty"), so don't get too bogged down in details. You continue:

You: That very night after the meeting, I went back to the intersection and did notice the "No Left Turn 4 p.m. to 6 p.m., Except Sunday & Holidays" along with 46 other directional signals or signs. I also noticed that "LOCO" was spray painted diagonally across the sign, obscuring part of the sign. This is the only one of the 47 signals or signs that states "NO LEFT TURN." Your honor, I'm fairly certain that it was before 4 o'clock when I made my turn because of the fact that I was seated for over five minutes prior to the ticket being issued. I have a diagram of the area.

You didn't get pictures because the intersection had changed since your ticket. You have to deal with what you've got, not what you would like to have.

Holmes: Objection.

Judge: Admitted into evidence. Anything further?

You: No, Your Honor.

Judge: Any questions by the People?

Seeking a little revenge (even though it's not allowed), Ms. Holmes has a grin on her face.

Holmes: Yes, Your Honor, just a few.

Holmes: There was a sign at the intersection stating "NO LEFT TURN," correct?

You're in Jones's shoes now.

You: Yes, but . . .

Holmes: Objection-beyond the word, "Yes".

Judge: Sustained. Just answer the question.

Holmes: The first time you looked at a clock it was 4:05 p.m., correct?

You: Yes, but . . .

Holmes: Objection, beyond the word, "Yes".

Judge: Sustained.

Holmes: You did make a left turn, correct?

You: Yes, but . . .

Holmes: Objection.

Judge: Sustained.

Holmes: Nothing further, Your Honor.

Judge: Do you want to argue the case or submit it?

You: Your Honor, I'd like to further testify.

Judge: Denied, I've heard enough. Argument by the People?

In a system that functions primarily to make money for the state, you're just clogging things up.

Holmes: Your Honor, by the defendant's own admission, he turned left and there was a NO LEFT TURN sign posted. The Defendant is guilty.

Judge: Defense argument?

You say: Your Honor, first, there was no adequate notice as required by law that the left turn was prohibited, so the turn is a legal act without the sign posted. There are 47 different directional signals or signs at the intersection that have to be assimilated by a driver in the matter of seconds. It would be unreasonable to expect a driver to comprehend all the information in that time period. Therefore, there is no REASONABLE notice given to a driver of the violation of law. Without reasonable notice, there is no violation, and the Court should find Not Guilty.

           Second, the fact that the word LOCO was written across the sign voids the enforcement of the provision of the sign because only authorized and approved signs can be posted. Since we can assume that LOCO is not employed by the State to place his name on the sign, the fact that his name is there and conceals other information therefore voids the sign.

           Third, the sign only prohibits turns between 4

p.m. and 6 p.m. The testimony from the officer clearly shows that he writes the time at the end of the citation, 1610 on this one. The officer also admits that he took approximately five minutes to issue the citation and that his watch is set five minutes fast, so the time of the occurrence could have been before 4 pm, therefore not in violation of the prohibited act.

Finally, the sign excepts Sundays and Holidays. The date of 2–15–93 was President's Day, a national holiday. Therefore, the act did not violate the posted sign.

Thank you for your consideration in this matter. For the foregoing reasons, the defendant is entitled to a Verdict of Not Guilty.

Judge: Anything further?

You: No.

Holmes: Will submit . . .

Judge: Court Verdict—"GUILTY."

$108 and 1 point poorer, you just barely catch the 6:48 p.m. flight out of town. Oh, well, you speeded to make the flight and didn't get caught.

We end this example this way to emphasize perspective. You did a great job of preparation, you embarrassed the legal system, and you even forced the judge to act imprudently. Sure, you're out the $108, but you can take heart in affirming, if only to yourself, that you're the winner . . . or did I mean **A WINNER**?

Chapter Ten

THE UNEXPECTED

I am going to make a bold claim that will establish "foundation" for you to read this chapter.

My law practice is very rare in that I specialize exclusively in traffic ticket defense. In the last, oh, say five years, I have tried more cases than any other attorney in America, with the possible exception of my partner John Farris. It's not necessarily by my choosing that I hold this distinction. It's because the very nature of the traffic ticket system that we talked about in Chapter 1 is based on quantity.

That's unfortunate for many of the victims of that system, but for you it offers a wealth of twists and turns that come along with a perverted legal system. Let's look at a few of the more interesting and bizarre cases (California Code citations, unless otherwise noted) that will help you understand how this really works. They may also give some hints as to unexpected opportunities or dangers for you.

The cases are grouped according to the violation categories in Chapter 9:

Speeding Tickets

Speeding Example #1—Radar

Facts: "Mrs. B" on a four-lane road got a radar speeding ticket for going 47 in a 35 zone. Cop testified to no traffic in front of or behind Mrs. B. It was a clear, dry day.

Citation: Citation 22350: City cop cited Mrs. B for unsafe speed.

Law: "No person shall drive a vehicle upon a highway at a speed greater than is reasonable or prudent having due regard for weather, visibility, the traffic on . . ."

Defense Argument: Although the 35 mph posted creates a presumption of a safe and reasonable speed, in these circumstances 47 mph was a safe speed given the factors of weather, traffic, etc.

Verdict: Court found Mrs. B "Not Guilty" because she was "traveling at a safe speed." Defense attorney one of the most shocked people in the courtroom.

Lesson: Just goes to show that you really don't have anything to lose. The case wasn't particularly strong, yet one time in one court, one judge said, "It makes sense to me." He never would have made that judgment if he hadn't been asked.

Speeding Example #2—Calibration

Facts: Officer followed defendant a short distance, then stopped and issued citation for driving 70 mph in a 45 mph zone.

Citation: Driving at unsafe speed, 70/45 (70 mph in 45 mph zone).

Defense Argument: After the prosecution finished their case ("People Rest"), defense noted that no speedometer calibration evidence was presented at trial.

Verdict: "Not Guilty." No foundation; officer relied solely on speedometer to issue ticket.

Lesson: Simple oversight on prosecution's part. Had we objected before they "rested," they could have fixed it. Instead, we let them lose their case for us.

Speeding Example #3—Pacing Flaws

Facts: Officer states that he establishes a visual pace, when entering freeway, of defendant's car at 55 mph. Defendant keeps out of pace range of cop, therefore defendant is going faster.

Citation: Exceeding the maximum speed; driving 65 mph in 55 mph zone.

Defense Argument: No foundation on speedometer. You could go 55.9 mph and be over 55 mph, but not in violation of the law.

Verdict: "Not Guilty." Defense "made sense" to the judge.

Lesson: Not much of a real defense here, but common sense really worked! In other words, the court bought it!

Speeding Example #4—Pace: The Sequel

Facts: Officer paces defendant's vehicle at 70/55.

Citation: Exceeding the maximum speed; 70/55.

Defense Argument: Cop testifies pace vehicle (his car) relied on accuracy of speedometer. We object as to foundation. Motion to strike his testimony as to accuracy of the speedometer.

Verdict: "Not Guilty." The officer had his documentation present, but did not offer it into evidence.

Lesson: Never underestimate the incompetence of a cop on the stand.

Speeding Example #5—Radar: The Sequel

Facts: Radar, properly qualified and calibrated, catches defendant in unposted area (default speed limit 55 mph). Officer also testifies that he was on duty, in uniform and in a marked vehicle.

Citation: Exceeding maximum speed; 65/55.

Defense Argument: No speed ever testified to by cop. He forgot to say how fast the car was going.

Verdict: "Not Guilty." Court had no choice, a crime hadn't been committed.

Lesson: Remember, you only have to win once. Have your checklist in front of you during the cop's testimony. If he only misses one, you win. This cop missed the best one!

Speeding Example #6—Calibration

Facts: Defendant caught driving at unsafe speed.

Citation: Unsafe speed.

Defense Argument: Officer testifies in court "A". Court gets busy with "important stuff", case sent to court "B", officer starts to testify again. Motion for dismissal. Jeopardy attached in Court "A"; case not completed. Double jeopardy attached in Court "B" when cop starts to testify.

Verdict: "Not Guilty." Double jeopardy applied.

Lesson: We had no idea we'd get this motion, but tried it anyway. What have you got to lose?

Speeding Example #7—Calibration: The Sequel

Facts: Radar ticket for 70 mph in a 55 mph zone. All other relevant data on scene was proper.

Citation: Exceeding maximum speed; 70/55.

Defense Argument: Officer stated at 70/55, no need for survey. Calibration of radar unit was available but not present. He also said that he would not have issued citation on visual alone.

Verdict: "Not Guilty." No foundation.

Lesson: A simple case of laziness on the prosecution's part. They really just thought they could get a conviction without following their own rules.

Speeding Example #8—Accuracy of Ticket

Facts: Cop wrote down 105 mph in the "approximate" box on _his_ ticket, but did not write anything in "approximate" box on Defendant's citation.

Citation: Unsafe speed; 100+ mph.

Defense Argument: 1) Altered ticket, therefore nonconforming copy with court. 2) Code requires that the speed be entered in box.

Verdict: "Not Guilty." No foundation.

Lesson: Don't throw away or mutilate your ticket. It's one more chance to let them lose their case against you.

Speeding Example #9—"People Rest"

Facts: Cop testifies that he was doing 70 mph following the defendant.

Citation: Unsafe speed; 70/55.

Defense Argument: No testimony as to what _defendant's_ car was doing. Cop said, "I was going 70 mph." He never said how fast the defendant's car was going.

Verdict: "Not Guilty." No evidence presented that implicated the defendant.

Lesson: Officer's testimony must directly accuse defendant of a crime. By waiting for the "people" to rest, the defendant can prevent the prosecution from correcting its error.

Speeding Example #10—"Safe" Speed

Facts: Posted 25 mph, but highway had six lanes with center divider; no traffic, no pedestrians, near beach area during winter day.

Citation: Unsafe speed; 40/25.

Defense Argument: Defense asked officer, "What would be the fastest safe speed for those conditions?" Officer replied, "40 mph."

Verdict: "Not Guilty." The officer cited for unsafe speed but admitted that under those particular circumstances 40 mph would be safe.

Lesson: Just because you exceeded the speed limit does not mean you're guilty of unsafe speed.

Speeding Example #11—Common Sense

Facts: Officer testified that defendant was ahead of him in the fast lane, with the officer in the slow lane on a busy freeway at 7:00 on a Friday night. Officer paced defendant for 1½ miles at 80 mph. Defendant never changed lanes and officer never changed lanes.

Citation: Unsafe speed; 80/55.

Defense Argument: Questioning caused doubt as to how both the officer and the defendant could speed at 80 mph in separate lanes without ever having to change lanes.

Verdict: "Not Guilty." Court didn't believe officer.

Lesson: Sometimes it's helpful to step back and try to see if the officer's testimony simply makes sense. This time it didn't.

Judgment Tickets

Judgment Example #1—Truck Lanes, I
Facts: Cop going in other direction, sees truck in first of three lanes (fast lane). Cop hangs U-turn and catches truck in middle lane. Cites for truck out of lane.

Citation: Truck out of lane.

Defense Argument: 1) Freeway intersection ahead—truck must be in middle lane to travel through. 2) Before cop sees truck, freeway goes from two to three lanes. The truck could have been out in fast lane legally, then third lane added to inside making his position illegal.

Verdict: "Not Guilty." Court bought location evidence.

Lesson: Detailed diagram revealed lane changes of freeway. Competent approach added credibility to other testimony.

Judgment Example #2—Lanes, II
Facts: Cop testifies truck in middle lane and should have pulled over when passed vehicle. Defendant present and testifies that he passed one truck and was about to pass another.

Citation: Truck out of lane.

Defense Argument: Trucks can be out in middle lane if passing slower vehicles—law does not require trucks to pull back in after every vehicle passed.

Verdict: "Not Guilty." Cop misinterpreted law.

Lesson: Read the law that you've been accused of violating.

Judgment Example #3—Blocked Intersection
Facts: Intersection was blocked but defendant entered on yellow light. Traffic was moving ahead of defendant but then stopped.

Citation: Blocking intersection.

Defense Argument: On cross-examination officer could not recall if there was a large truck in front of defendant.

Verdict: "Not Guilty." No reasonable notice that he couldn't clear intersection.

Lesson: With line of sight blocked by truck, benefit of doubt must go to defendant.

Judgment Example #4—Lights

Facts: The officer testified that the defendant was approaching him and failed to dim his high beams.

Citation: Failure to dim high beams.

Defense Argument: Officer forgot to testify that it was dark.

Verdict: "Not Guilty."

Lesson: You only have to win once.

Judgment Example #5—Turn Lane

This is an active case.

Facts: "Mr. A" on a six-lane road makes a U-turn into the center lane from a two-way left turn lane.

Citation: City cop cites "Mr. A" under Code 214605 for two-way left turn lanes.

Law: Cop cited under inappropriate 214605 Code section: "A vehicle shall not be driven in a designated two-way left-turn lane except when preparing for or making a left turn from or into a highway or when preparing for or making a U-turn when otherwise permitted by law . . ."

Defense Argument: There may very well have been a violation of law, but the fact of this auto turn was not an improper use of the center left or U-turn lane. The State must prove that the U-turn was illegal, not the use of the lane.

Lesson: Never assume the cop knows what he is doing. They write so many tickets for so many reasons that
their confusion and ambivalence can be your best
weapon.

Sign Tickets

Sign Example #1—Yield

Facts: Citation issued in conjunction with accident.
Cop, who did not witness the accident, was the only witness at trial.

Citation: Failure to yield.

Defense Argument: Cop was not present at scene
when accident occurred, therefore not an eyewitness to
the accident. He couldn't testify that defendant failed to
yield.

Verdict: "Not Guilty." Hearsay evidence.

Lesson: Cop must testify as to what he saw, not what
he heard from a witness.

Sign Example #2—Double Yellow

Facts: Defendant crossed over double-double yellow lines.

Citation: Crossing over double-double yellow lines.

Defense Argument: Width between double-double
must be two feet and established in People's case. People
failed to produce that evidence.

Verdict: "Not Guilty."

Lesson: All elements must be present for you to be
in violation. Make them produce all those facts.

Sign Example #3—Sky Goof

Facts: Defendant present. Helicopter pilot spots car
falling to yield. No questions on cross-examination.

Citation: Failure to yield.

Defense Argument: Defendant motion to dismiss—no identification of driver.

Verdict: "Not Guilty."

Lesson: Identification is *always* an issue.

Sign Example #4—Lanes

Facts: Cop said defendant ran red light.

Citation: Running red light.

Defense Argument: Defendant said he didn't run red.

Verdict: "Not Guilty." Factual judge believed defendant entered on yellow light.

Lesson: Occasionally, you can win these cop's-word-against-yours battles if your other evidence is solid.

Sign Example #5—Red Light/Green Light

Facts: Cop testified that he was going eastbound, and his light changed from red to green. He saw defendant, going northbound, enter intersection after cop's light turned green. Cited for red light.

Citation: Red light violation.

Defense Argument: No testimony as to what color the light was for the Defendant.

Verdict: "Not Guilty."

Lesson: Everything may seem obvious, then the prosecution forgets that you have to be accused of something.

Non-Moving Tickets

Non-Moving Example #1—No Habla Español.

Facts: Ran check on driver, no valid license appeared. Didn't recall if defendant was Spanish-speaking.

Officer doesn't speak Spanish.

Citation: Unlicensed driver.

Defense Argument: Hispanics commonly use two last names. Cop didn't run second last name.

Verdict: "Not Guilty." Validation in place.

Lesson: Don't let simple mistakes on the court's part intimidate you. It's their fault.

Non-Moving Example #2—FTA

Facts: Hispanic defendant fails to appear for court date.

Citation: Failure to appear.

Defense Argument: Officer didn't recall if defendant was Spanish-speaking. Officer doesn't speak Spanish. No notice in Spanish to defendant.

Verdict: "Not Guilty." No proper notice.

Lesson: You must be able to understand the accusations.

Non-Moving Example #3—Equipment

Facts: Officer testified that he cited the defendant for a car that had tinted windows and no registration.

Citation: Tinted windows and no registration.

Defense Argument: Foundation; there were no "facts" as to what the officer saw, heard or felt—only the citation.

Verdict: "Not Guilty."

Lesson: Don't be intimidated by hearsay evidence, even if it comes from a cop.

Non-Moving Example #4—"Fix-it" Tickets

Facts: Cop stops "Mr. C" for expired registration (no sticker on license plate).

Citation: City cop cited Mr. C for "Registration not Valid."

Law: Code 4000: "No person shall drive, move, or leave standing upon a highway . . . any motor vehicle . . . unless it is REGISTERED and the appropriate fees have been paid under this code section . . ."

Defense Argument: 1) That Mr. C *had* the car registered to him. There was no evidence by the people to prove whether or not the fees had been paid. 2) There was a more specific charge for the facts. "That it was unlawful not to display the sticker." Therefore, not a violation of 4000a, nor was the complaint amended to charge the correct violation.

Verdict: "Not Guilty." But the fine for the correct charge was one-third what it should have been because "the cop was doing Mr. C a favor."

Lesson: This is a good one to "feel good" about. We proved our point and reduced the overall liability.

Chapter Eleven

HIRING A FAST GUN (AND KEEPING IT POINTED IN THE RIGHT DIRECTION)

T here is a simple rule to start with here, especially if this is the first chapter that you're reading.

> *Consult with an attorney in any case where jail time is at issue.*

When will jail time become an issue? This is by no means a complete list (some judges might throw you in jail "jus' 'cause"), but here is the official "I'd Better Call Someone" Test to determine when you may need help (check all that apply).

"I'd Better Call Someone If My Case Involves:"

_____ Driving under the influence of alcohol.

_____ Driving on a suspended license.

_____ Reckless driving.

_____ Hit and run driving.

_____ Possibly a case involving an accident.

_____ Any felony in which your car or your driving may have been involved (drug possession, robbery, etc.)

When jail time is involved, you will also have a right to a court-appointed attorney, if you can't afford one.

When the infraction is not punishable by jail time, you still have the option to retain (hire) counsel. But even though they're on your side, there are some real issues that you need to consider. I should know, I'm one of those attorneys.

When It's Smart, When It's Not.

Noble motives aside, the first job of a private attorney is to get your money out of your pocket and into his. He is a business man, and his business is representing the client.

First, ask yourself if you really *need* an attorney or just *want* an attorney. This is a decision that doesn't have a "right" or "wrong" answer to it, just (you hope) a "best" answer under the circumstances. In coming to your decision, ask yourself:

1) What are the options available to me?

a) Traffic School (Good if you HAVE TO WIN).

b) Trial (May be your only viable option).

c) Plead guilty/forfeit bail (BAD OPTION ALWAYS).

With answers "A" and "C", you don't need an attorney. You can do those by mail.

"B", Trial, is the *only* reason you should consider an attorney.

2) What are the ramifications of losing a ticket?

a) A point on your DMV record.

b) Insurance rates go up.

Call your agent and ask a hypothetical question: "What if someone got this (whatever) kind of ticket? Would his rates go up, and by how much?" The rate difference might be less than the attorney's fees.

c) Loss of license.

d) Jail. (Very unlikely.)

Calculate the cost factor against the chance of success with an attorney versus your chance of success without one.

Through the last six years and over 2,000 cases, we have won over 60% of all cases. Between 33⅓% and 40% of those wins came from cases being dismissed because of Lack of Prosecution (The cop doesn't show.)

Of the approximately 60% of cases that did go to trial, 25% were won on the inability of the prosecution to prove their case. Only about 10% have been won on an affirmative defense. Either the law or the court believes the defendant and renders a verdict of NOT GUILTY. So your best chance of winning the case is to show up and hope like hell the cop doesn't.

Secondly, consider the chance of the prosecution's inability to prove their case against you. This is probably the best type of case in which to have an attorney represent you. Your attorney can prevent the prosecution from getting some pieces of evidence in.

Finally, if it comes to a credibility issue, you will normally be equally credible with or without an attorney. The advantage is that an attorney will be able, through questions and answers, to lead you through your testimony. However, he or she will have little control over your cross-examination by the prosecution.

An attorney will be more familiar with courtroom procedure and rules of evidence. He will be able to analyze the issues in the case and formulate a coherent argument. He will be able to get evidence introduced properly and effectively cross-examine witnesses on the other side. He should lower your anxiety and stress levels.

An attorney can represent your interest without you even being present at the trial. Your time and energy are valuable assets, and an attorney can save you both.

Use an attorney to your benefit—just as you would a plumber (lots of similarities) or a mechanic (same reputation)—to do a job that you COULD do if you had the time and energy, but that you'd rather leave to a qualified person so you don't have to get messy.

However, like the other professions, attorneys come at a price, and it is that price versus your consequences that should determine if you WANT to hire an attorney.

Besides cost, there are some other possible disadvantages of hiring an attorney. Most attorneys don't specialize in this small and relatively insignificant area of law. They may do it for you as a favor because you are a good client. They may not have much time (because of the low fee) to devote to the case. The court will presume that if you are represented by an attorney, you will have been informed of all your rights and waive (give up) those rights not specifically retained.

Remember, a key advantage of representing yourself is that you know your own case better than anyone else in the WORLD, guaranteed. No one will care more about you or your case than you. Use that to your advantage. At trial you get to play the dual role of an attorney and a witness. This is actually a wonderful opportunity that you could use to your advantage, putting the other side at a disadvantage.

The police officer can't act as an attorney for the prosecution, and the prosecutor can't be a witness in the case. You, on the other hand, can do both. With the right attitude a trial can be enjoyable, as long as you keep everything in perspective.

In 90% of the cases, as long as you don't testify and convict yourself, there is little or no advantage to hiring an attorney. The trouble is that there's no real way to know which cases fall in the other 10% until *after* the trial.

Chapter Twelve

WHEN IT'S OVER . . .

I t's over.

It's really that simple. If you won, go kiss your wife/husband/boyfriend/girlfriend, whatever.

If you lost, do the same thing and move on with your life.

We have stressed throughout this book the value of the trial experience well beyond just fighting the traffic ticket. If you let the incompetence and arrogance of the cop, D.A. and/or judge get to you after the trial, you may start to lose perspective.

Of course, feelings of anger and frustration immediately after a "Guilty" verdict are completely logical. You just went through maybe a month's worth of preparations, complete with charts, pictures and prepared testimony. You pinned the cop's testimony to the wall, and you handled all the D.A.'s questions with ease. Everything was on your side . . . except the Verdict.

IT'S NOT FAIR.

If that's the way you feel, then good . . . for about five minutes. Remember Chapter 1? "Fair" is a concept that doesn't always prevail in court. Take what you've learned and go forward, because it will only be of value if you learn to let go.

Okay, okay, if you still want to go on, you do have the right to file an appeal. But the only obvious exception to this "move on" rule is if the consequences of not filing an appeal are truly serious. And if the stakes were really that high, you probably should have hired an attorney in the first place.

You might think that the only other reason to pursue the case is that you lost your temper in court and punched the judge. Unfortunately, even a reversal of your traffic ticket on appeal will have nothing to do with the problems you will have created by assaulting an officer of the court.

Enough said. You are smart enough to have come this far, and therefore you are smart enough to have realized the true benefit of learning how to fight the system.

Along the way, you may even have won your case.

Index

BONUS BOOKS FOR CARS AND DRIVERS

The Safe Motorist's Guide to Speedtraps
State-by-state listings to keep drivers out of trouble
John Tomerlin and Dru Whitledge
ISBN 0-929387-26-0
367 pages—$19.95 paper

Beating the Radar Rap
**Tested techniques for fighting
electronic speed entrapment**
Dale T. Smith and John Tomerlin
ISBN 0-933893-89-2
160 pages—$14.95 paper

Used Cars: Finding the Best Buy
**"An excellent advice and selection guide"
—ALA Booklist**
Jim Mateja
ISBN 0-933893-52-3
208 pages—$6.95 paper

Recreational Vehicles
**Everything you need to know
about buying an RV**
Bill Alderman, Jr., and Eleanore Wilson
ISBN 0-933893-78-7
128 pages—$6.95 paper

160 East Illinois Street
Chicago, Illinois 60611
(800) 225-3775